Rainbow Technology

Techniques for Primary Design and Technology

Chris Gibson
Jean Harding
Janet Hutchings
John Mapstone
Brian Pengelly

Stanley Thornes (Publishers) Ltd

First published in 1991 by
Stanley Thornes (Publishers) Ltd
Old Station Drive
Leckhampton
CHELTENHAM GL53 0DN, UK.

British Library Cataloguing in Publication Data

Techniques for primary design and technology.
  — (Rainbow technology)
  I. Gibson, Chris   II. Series
  372.3

  ISBN 0-7487-1123-6

Typeset by Tech-Set, Gateshead, Tyne & Wear.
Printed in Great Britain at The Bath Press, Avon.

Contents

How to use this book

Techniques for Primary Design and Technology is a photocopiable resource of basic techniques and skills for Key Stages 1 and 2. It can be used either on its own or alongside the other Rainbow Technology components. It covers a wide range of essential techniques for the construction of working, moving models in a step-by-step form. The aim is to provide a substantial bank of ideas useful both for teachers approaching technology for the first time and for those looking for slightly more advanced techniques. These techniques concentrate on the aspects of technology which seem to cause most concern to primary school teachers. These aspects include making models and prototypes which require pulleys, gears and motors as well as the use of electricity and mechanisms. It is, however, important to remember that technology is not just 'wheels and gears'. Textiles, food and graphic media are also important areas of technological activity highlighted in the programmes of study. We have not covered them here for reasons of space and because of their slightly greater familiarity to primary school teachers. You will find that the Rainbow Technology Context Cards provide wide-ranging opportunities for their exploration.

This book provides 104 photocopiable sheets in 12 sections, accompanied by teacher's notes and technological challenges. The sections are as follows:

- Electricity – the basics of electricity: electrical components, circuits, switches and lights

- Structures – how to make simple structures both for models and at full size out of wood, paper, card and Corriflute

- Going round and round – how to make wheels, axles, tyres, pulleys, gears, winches and turntables

- Making noises – how to create some noise-making machines

- Motors – how to make simple non-electric motors

- Releasing – ways of triggering and releasing devices

- Making adjustments – how to adjust devices

- Mechanisms – levers, couplings, cranks, connecting rods, cams and eccentrics

- Pneumatics and hydraulics – how to make, adjust and use hydraulic systems

- Fastening – ideas for fixing and hinging materials

- Photography – how to make a type of pinhole camera

- A home-made construction set – how to create a simple construction set for making models and structures that need strong frameworks, out of very basic materials.

The sheets are intended for dual use: either by teachers, as a resource for their own use, or to put directly in front of children. For this reason the sheets have been written in step-by-step pictorial form with few words and uncomplicated instructions. It is likely that teachers at Key Stage 1 will want to extract ideas from the sheets to present to children themselves; Key Stage 2 children may be able to follow up ideas more directly.

You will find that the sheets provide activities and strategies that underwrite the content of the programmes of study at Key Stages 1 and 2 in the four areas:

Developing and using artefacts, systems and environments;
Working with materials;
Developing and communicating ideas;
Satisfying needs and addressing opportunities.

A considerable amount of help is given with work on systems (particularly control and the use of mechanisms), energy and structures; on working with materials (particularly the suitability of materials and joining materials); on ways of communicating ideas and on evaluating and modifying work done.

An underlying aim of these sheets is to try to avoid presenting what might be called 'recipe technology', i.e. prescriptive instructions for making particular artefacts to arrive at predetermined results. Such directed activities have little or nothing to do with real technology, which is defined by Technology in the National Curriculum as 'identifying and fulfilling real needs and opportunities'. Instead, the sheets aim to give support without determining outcomes and to provide the basic building blocks of technical knowledge so that children can find solutions to problems generated by themselves. For this reason the sheets very largely avoid suggesting particular applications. For example, a pressure pad is an excellent device for making a burglar alarm, but it also has many other uses. Rather than produce a sheet entitled 'How to make a burglar alarm', we have tried to avoid over-specific suggestions which can only lead to predetermined outcomes. Often, different techniques will need to be combined in order to solve a problem. A child who wants to construct a motorised fire engine with coloured flashing lights would draw widely on techniques in the sections on Electricity, Structures, Going round and round, Motors and Making adjustments.

You will find that the techniques often provide more than one way of solving a problem; for example, two different ways of controlling fluid flow in a hydraulic system are presented. The aim here is to provide choice and an element of progression in techniques. It cannot be stressed too strongly that Design and Technology is about selecting and choosing widely within the experience and knowledge of an individual child. There is rarely a 'correct' answer to a problem. It is important for children to develop their knowledge and skills in choosing with the teacher's help.

It is hoped that you and your pupils will use the sheets flexibly in this way as a resource for open-ended problem solving. There may, of course, be occasions when you want to focus on a specific technique for some reason; for example, if you are studying electricity and conductivity in science you might want to make up the simple circuit tester on Sheet 4. By and large, however, we hope that you will use the sheets in response to real needs generated by children in the classroom. In order to help you see the potential of many of the techniques we have mentioned possible applications in the teacher's notes at the front of the book and also include an index of applications. You will also find a short list of challenges for each set of teacher's notes; these are opportunities for children to solve defined problems using the techniques within a section. In the teacher's notes reference is made to the techniques as suggestions for solving problems on the Context Cards.

Teacher's notes

These notes provide further information about using the sheets, and ideas for applications of the techniques shown. You will not find notes for every sheet, as a considerable number are self-explanatory.

Electricity

2 Simple electrical components and materials 2

A reed switch is useful when you need a switch which can be operated without being touched. The magnet will work the switch from up to 1 cm away. It is useful for burglar alarms on doors, to create hidden switches that can only be operated by a hand-held magnet or with moving vehicles such as buggies or trains: if a magnet is fixed to the vehicle, a circuit can be completed as the vehicle passes the reed switch at a certain point.

Reed switches are delicate components, so it may be sensible to protect a reed switch assembly by a short length of plastic tube.

3 Simple electrical components and materials 3

A microswitch requires only a very light pressure on the metal lever to make it work. Its sensitivity makes it useful as an obstacle detector on a moving vehicle: when the vehicle bumps into something the switch can be wired to cut out the motor or sound a warning. It could be used to stop a model lift at each floor. With a suitable pad attached to the lever it can be used to sense rainfall: as the water gathers on the pad, the switch will sink until the circuit is completed and a warning sent out about the weather.

When using the hand drill to coil two or three wires together it is important that the wires are stretched out reasonably tautly to avoid sagging.

4 Making circuits

The simple continuity or circuit tester can be used to investigate conduction and insulation of materials. A lovely practical use of this was suggested by a six-year-old who made a robot with teeth made from two pieces of aluminium foil used in place of the drawing pins in the diagram. When the robot was fed 'metallic food', its eyes lit up because the food bridged the gap between the teeth and completed the circuit.

6 Symbols for electrical circuits

Children should start to use electrical symbols at Key Stage 2 as part of the core programme of study for developing and communicating ideas.

9 Making electrical connections 2

When using a ball-bearing connector you can use a marble wrapped in aluminium foil in place of the ball bearing. Similarly, foil stuck down with glue can be used instead of copper strips. The pieces of foil should be separated by a small gap of less than 2 mm. This connector is useful in dexterity games where a rolling ball is steered round or into holes, or, at the end of a runway along which the ball has been moving as part as a timing activity. It could also be used to form part of a scoring system on a pinball or bagatelle type of toy: when the ball falls into the hole, the circuit is completed and a score is registered by a buzzer or light.

The hidden connections mean that it is not possible to see which two holes in the top card have to be touched by the probes to make a circuit. In this way matching activities or quizzes can be created. The holes can be labelled with words, some of which form matching pairs. If the probes are put into the correct holes matching, say, acorn and oak, then the bulb lights to show a correct response. Juniors could devise such matching activities for infants; trees and fruit, colours and their names, flags and countries are some of many possibilities. The pad can have many more holes and possible connections than are shown in the sketch.

10 Slide switches

The change-over switch is useful to switch something off and something else on immediately afterwards. For example, on a darkroom door there might be light-up signs saying 'In use' and 'Available'. When someone goes in, they can use a change-over switch to turn off the 'Available' sign and light up the 'In use' sign straightaway. In a more complex situation two such switches can be connected to create a model of an upstairs-downstairs two-way light-switching circuit in which a light can be switched on and off from both downstairs and upstairs. The change-over switch is used as shown in Figure 1. A brassed paper fastener is an alternative way of fixing the lolly stick to the board.

Provided that the lolly stick is always touching one of the two drawing pins in each switch, the switch will work.

11 Press switches

The press-to-make switch can be used as a morse code tapper or bell push for a doll's house. The press-to-break switch is the reverse and could be used as an emergency stop switch in a model machine.

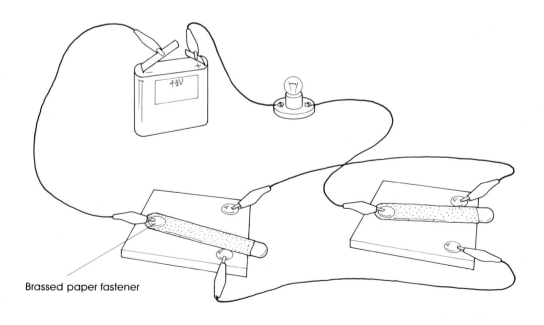

Brassed paper fastener

Figure 1

12 Reversing switches

When making reversing switches ensure that the drawing pins line up against the side of the lolly stick when it is moved from one side to the other. It is easy to understand how a reversing switch works once it has been made and the flow of electricity followed.

13 Making switches from everyday items 1

When making the peg switch you will need dowel of about 6 mm or ¼ inch diameter. If you use double-sided sticky tape, make sure the wood is completely dry and dust free. It may also help to tape the wires to the broad flat surfaces of the pegs so that the risk of accidental damage is minimised.

15-17 Switches that turn 1-3

Switches that turn are useful in creating flashing lights, for example, on a lighthouse or advertising sign. Pulleys from an electric motor can be used to turn the switch. Hazard warning and indicator lights on buggies or Lego® models are also exciting. The various switches represent a progression in level of difficulty of manufacture. They also lead on naturally to programmable switches which most children will not be ready to approach until year 5 or 6. However, these switches can form the basis of a simple, cheap demonstration of automation if the disc is turned by a motor or hand-turned pulley system.

18 A programmable switch

Because this switch allows several pairs of wires to be connected by aluminium foil patches at varying times, it is possible to arrange several switching operations automatically. An example is shown in Figure 2.

19-22 A pressure pad/Membrane switches 1-3

The pressure pad and membrane switch depend for sensitivity on the size of the hole in the foam or of the middle card in the sandwich. Foam is more robust and will survive heavy usage longer than card. The multi-way membrane panel can be used to form the basis of a control panel.

23-4 Tilt switches 1 and 2

Tilt switches are useful for burglar alarms. A simple bicycle alarm could be designed so that when the bike is moved an alarm is triggered. For the pivot tilt switch, pivot positions are shown above and below the switch. When the pivot is below, the switch is extremely sensitive to very slight movements and may prove temperamental.

25 Light sources using a battery

Light-emitting diodes will prove some exciting additions to a Lego® model. The standard 5 mm type fits neatly into the holes in Lego® Tecnik. They can be used to make model traffic lights, or the red ones can make stop lights and the amber, warning or indicator lights on vehicles. If you use more than one LED then you may find that you have to reduce the value of the 150 ohm resistor or even do without one altogether. Be aware that LEDs only work if correctly connected to the battery: connected one way they will not light. Simply reconnect them the opposite way and they should glow brightly. In order to calculate the correct resistor value, use the following formula.

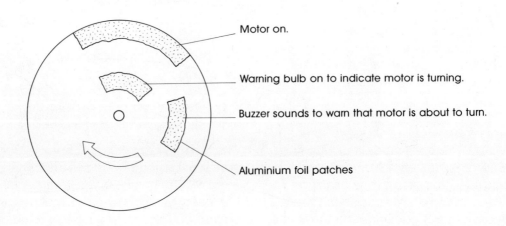

Motor on.

Warning bulb on to indicate motor is turning.

Buzzer sounds to warn that motor is about to turn.

Aluminium foil patches

Figure 2

If the battery voltage is 4.5 volts and the resistor has a value of R, then

$$R = \frac{1000}{20}(4.5 - 1.2)$$

$$R = 50 \times 3.3$$

$$R = 165 \text{ ohms}$$

The nearest value available would probably be 150 ohms. For other battery sizes simply change the 4.5 value in the equation.

28 Logic circuits

Logic-switching systems are useful where sequences of switches are necessary. For example, on a model washing machine one switch could be on the door and the other on the start switch. Only if the one AND the other are used will the washing machine work. Alternatively, for a light operated from two switches you could use one OR the other to operate the light.

Structures

30-1 Testing structures for strength 1 and 2

These paper-folding activities can be used to learn about the relationship between materials and their form. Modifying sheet materials by simple folding gives much better load-carrying properties or impact-resisting qualities. A combination of tubes and bridge shapes can produce basic building forms as used in modern warehousing and school buildings.

32-5 Frameworks for models 1-4

Wooden frameworks are a natural progression from work with paper folding. They are much stronger structures which rely for joining techniques and strength on the sandwich of card triangles with the wood between them. It is the sandwich effect which is absolutely essential. Card on one side only is comparatively weak. These simple frameworks are very strong and can be used to produce models of buildings, bridges and vehicles, as well as parts of mechanisms used, for example, in a fairground ride. (Fairgrounds are an enormously fruitful source of activity for modelling structures and mechanisms.)

36-7 Frameworks from shadows 1 and 2

The shadow method has proved very effective with top infants, as they can cut out the card shape that suits their idea and then just cut wood to fit around the edge of the shape. This is easier for young children both to visualise and to handle. However, the sandwich is still crucial and small pieces of card must be glued on the inside of the frame. Do not take the actual shadow projection idea too literally. The shadow gives the idea of a silhouette but tends to have woolly edge definition. It does, however, help children to visualise one side of a three-dimensional object as a flat surface.

38-40 An outdoor stand/Adjustable stands

The outdoor stand ideas have uses for bird tables, race finishing markers, short flag poles, etc. They are not intended to be strong enough to carry heavy weights or to be climbed on!

41-4 Joining Corriflute 1-3/Pivoting and hinging Corriflute

Corriflute is supplied in different thicknesses. Sheets up to 3 mm thick are easy to cut using strong scissors. The thicker sheets of about 4.5 mm are quite tough and need a sharp knife and Maun safety rule. Corriflute is easy to fold in one direction and hard to bend at right angles to this. It is quite an expensive material, but if used appropriately it does become cost effective. It is ideal for large, stiff flat surfaces and for hinged applications such as lifting bridges.

Going round and round

46-7 Rolling along 1 and 2

If your pupils choose to punch holes in a box for their axles then alignment across the box can be a problem. The straw method was suggested by a seven-year-old and does help to achieve accuracy. However, if you need access to the axle for attaching a pulley or elastic band then a slot has to be cut in the box and the straw.

The basic buggy idea on Sheet 47 can be converted or customised to suit a particular design need. Alternatively, if you remove the wheels but keep the elastic-band motor you have a power house for a range of model-making purposes.

Cutting the notch in the disc on the axle is easily done with a Shapersaw (Model 1010). The crucial thing is to make the sides of the notch parallel, not V-shaped. This is quite tricky and might have to be done by an adult in the case of infants. The disc is best made from plywood.

52-3   Axles and spindles 1 and 2

Axles and spindles rotate many times in use, with the consequence that the holes in which they are located tend to wear away. One simple solution is to line up the card axle supports and glue them on, and then make a simple form of bearing. This could be a short length of plastic straw of about 5 mm diameter. The dowel rod will turn freely inside the straw as shown in Figure 3.

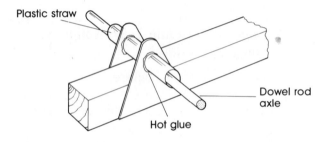

Plastic straw

Dowel rod axle

Hot glue

Figure 3

The straw can be held in place with a spot of glue from a hot glue gun.

54-5   Pulleys and belts/Pulleys and power

Pulleys are easy to make and can be used to reduce motor speed and increase turning power considerably. Using the complex pulley system, a model can be built that will transport at least three litres of PVA glue in their plastic bottles. This will give some idea of the power than can be generated by the careful use of an appropriate mechanical system.

Speed reduction can be illustrated using a simple calculation. Consider a simple pulley system with an electric motor driving the smaller pulley. If the motor turns at 2500 rpm and the pulley diameters are 1 cm and 10 cm respectively, then the speed of the larger pulley is found by multiplying the speed of the motor by the ratio of the pulley diameters.

i.e. The speed of the large pulley is

$$2500 \times \tfrac{1}{10} = 250 \text{ rpm.}$$

If the pulleys are swapped so that the larger one is on the motor, then the speed of the small pulley is

$$2500 \times \tfrac{1}{10} = 25\,000 \text{ rpm.}$$

The big difference between the two systems is that the first gives quite a lot of power to the larger pulley while the second gives almost no power to the smaller pulley.

In the complex pulley system, if you allow the pulleys to be the same size as above and replace the crank handle with a motor then the speed of the final pulley (labelled 'Driven'), will be equal to $2500 \times \tfrac{1}{10} \times \tfrac{1}{10}$ rpm. (Remember there are two pairs of pulleys.) This is only about 25 rpm but gives much more power to do useful work. The actual rpm is never exactly as calculated here because there are frictional losses within the system. If the complex pulley system is made as a model then you have a power house or simple engine that can be converted into a buggy, egg whisk, electric drill or crane winch depending on how the final output axle is connected.

57-9   Making gears 1-3

Gears are quite difficult to make and are probably best left to top juniors, although within every class there may be younger children who are well able to make use of gears. In any case, it can be an interesting activity to use a trammel to try to divide a disc into a number of equal sectors. If you have problems you can always use the gear templates. Gears are non-slip devices, unlike pulleys, so if you have need of a non-slip feature in a power system for a model, then gears are worthwhile. For instance, you may have a pupil modelling an historic machine such as a ballista and choosing to modify it by adding gearing to tension the machine with less human effort. A small gear turned by direct human effort driving a larger gear on the winch part of the mechanism is more efficient. This is shown in Figure 4 (opposite).

60   Gear templates

The gear templates may be photocopied and stuck on to card. The teeth can be glued on the radial lines to ensure exactly equal distances between them.

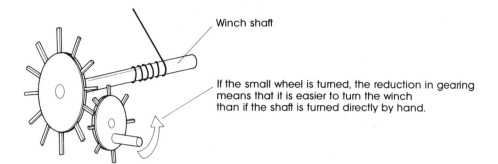

Winch shaft

If the small wheel is turned, the reduction in gearing means that it is easier to turn the winch than if the shaft is turned directly by hand.

Figure 4

62–3 Turntables 1 and 2

Turntables are useful in models for fairground rides, machinery for production lines in factories, railway turntables and mobile signs and displays in shop windows.

64 Making turntables turn

The speed ratio in the motorised turntable is about 30 cm : 0.1 cm or 300 : 1. Using a motor of speed 2500 rpm the speed of the turntable is about 8 rpm on a very simple system. In practice, frictional losses will modify the accuracy of the calculation.

Making noises

65–6 Noise makers/Noises from stretched fibres

Noise makers can be fun in their own right for young children. They can also serve a practical purpose in an alarm system, a bird–scaring machine (especially if linked to the programmable switch on Sheet 18) or a music machine.

Motors

67 Simple motors

Mention was made earlier of a power house (see notes on Pulleys and belts on p. 6). The vertical engine is also a power house but for lightweight power provision only — a fan or an advertising sign, perhaps. The elastic band is a cheap source of energy but its delivery of energy is slightly delayed through the complex pulley system. Depending on the accuracy of manufacture and the type of elastic band chosen, it may be necessary to put the winding

handle on the axle that the string is wound around. Experience has shown that the most effective elastic band is the long thin variety.

Releasing

71 Release and trigger mechanisms 1

Release and trigger mechanisms encourage fair testing of energy control devices. The wooden release, slightly modified, could form part of a catapult system for launching paper aeroplanes. The Lego® release can be used similarly.

72 Release and trigger mechanisms 2

Flowing water or dry sand can introduce the idea of timing to a trigger mechanism. With a little ingenuity both systems could be modified to empty when full up, so restarting the timing sequence and switching off the output. The output could go to a bulb, buzzer or motor. The water method could be linked to a weather topic related to assessing the amount of rainfall. For children at Level 5 the output could be fed into a computer control system such as 'Control It' or 'Sense It' (from RESOURCE) and a graphical output obtained of rainfall against time.

73 Release and trigger mechanisms 3

The rolling marble provides a much simpler timing device. The length and steepness of the chute or trough along which the marble rolls controls the speed of delivery. By changing either the length or steepness, different times can be obtained. Alternatively, if the opening of a door starts the marble rolling then another type of alarm system, with delayed action, is possible.

75 One-way turning

The one-way turning device (commonly known as a ratchet and pawl) is useful for winding devices such as a crane winch drum or well windlass. In everyday life one-way turning is used on winches and fishing reels.

Making adjustments

76 Sliding

These sliding systems are useful when you want something to return automatically. Some examples are shown in Figure 5.

77–8 Adjustable ladders 1 and 2

The ladder works very smoothly but is complex to make, so may best be attempted by older juniors. It may be incorporated into fire engines and street lighting repair vans.

79 Remote control linkages

The remote control linkage is useful in large constructions when various parts need to be operated but are hard to access. Suitable situations might be the points on a model railway layout or the raising of a level crossing barrier. Remote control linkages are also useful in a puppet theatre where various parts need to be moved by an operator who remains out of sight.

The rocking bar has a major place in history as the invention that enabled the draining of the Dutch polders. It has application in any system where force has to be applied around a corner. It could be part of a model railway signal operating system.

Mechanisms

80 Levers in models 1

This simple pendulum is easy to make. If you use a large paper clip, it is possible to set it

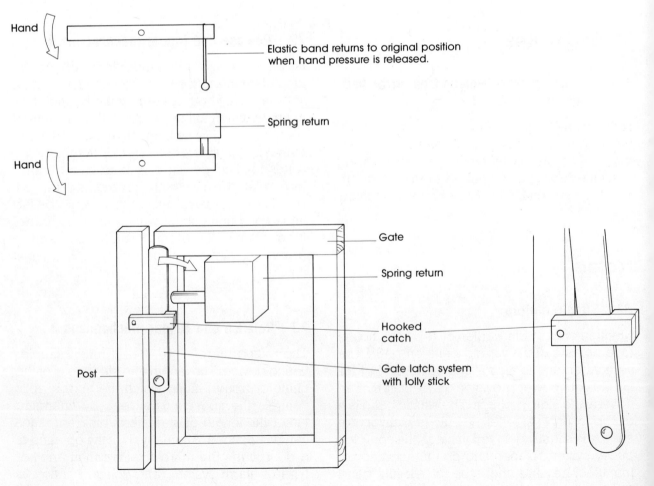

Figure 5

swinging to reproduce the tick-tock of a clock. The only difficulty is in the assembly, which needs long, thin fingers.

81   Levers in models 2

The brake in this model needs careful manufacture and may require modification using thick card. A pad of some material such as foam or leather on the end where it bears on the axle will improve control.

82   Levers in models 3

For both these models it is important that the holes for the paper fasteners are cleanly punched. The use of a Maun paper drill is recommended.

83   Simple mechanisms 1

The moving arm system could be used in simple robots or puppets. Automata or toys with moving parts could also make use of these systems.

84–6   Simple mechanisms 2–4

Cranks are extremely useful. If one or more connecting rods are taken from a single crank out through the sides of a box then models such as frogs or insects on the ends of the connecting rods can appear to jump about. Alternatively, the crank could move the arm of a figure holding a watering can in a model for the nursery rhyme 'Mary, Mary quite contrary'.

87–8   Cams and eccentrics 1 and 2

An eccentric is a circular disc mounted on an axle so that the axle is not at the centre of the disc, as shown in Figure 6.

A cam is a shaped piece of flat material that is anything other than circular. Figure 7 shows some examples.

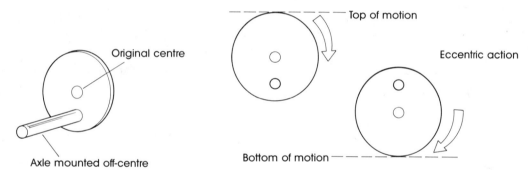

Figure 6

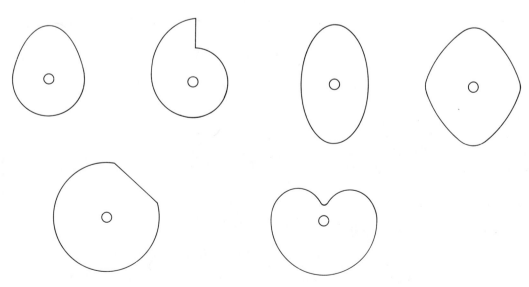

Figure 7

9

Both cams and eccentrics tend to be in close contact with a lever or plunger known as a follower. The follower moves in relation to the cam or eccentric as it is turned; see Figure 8.

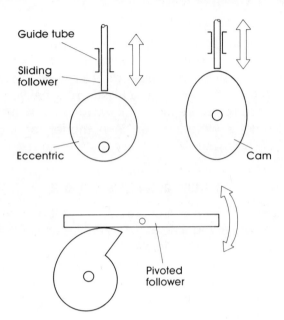

Figure 8

If the follower is above the cam or eccentric it will press downwards due to the influence of gravity. If it is in some other position then a spring or elastic band will be needed to keep the follower in contact with the cam or eccentric.

Cams and eccentrics are used to cause a change in direction and application of motion. In Figure 9, the eccentric goes around and the follower goes up and down, thus changing circular motion into linear motion.

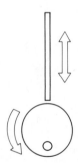

Figure 9

The cam in Figure 10 can only be turned one way. The follower rises slowly and drops rapidly when point A gets back to its start position.

Eccentrics are much easier for primary-aged children to make and use, although the snail cam is interesting as a contrast to the eccentric. The various methods of manufacture shown are simply to demonstrate some of the wide range of possibilities.

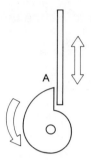

Figure 10

When a cam follower needs to slide freely, the use of a jumbo-sized plastic straw is recommended. The straw is easily secured to a box top by using a hot glue gun. These devices cannot be properly understood unless they are made and investigated. It may be appropriate to make up some of these models yourself and have them on display in the classroom for children to investigate.

Pneumatics and hydraulics

90 Making pneumatic and hydraulic systems 1

When using large and small syringes, useful sizes for each are 20 ml and 5 ml.

92 Using a pneumatic or hydraulic system

Syringes can add excitement to models in all sorts of ways. The spider can be made to pop out of a cardboard box, a sun or cloud could move in the sky, and a red balloon over a large syringe can give the impression of a moving tongue in an animal's or monster's head.

93 Adjusting hydraulic systems

The self-returning system has applications in Jack-in-the-box models. It can also be linked to a scissors-type mechanism to make a grab or gripper device as shown in Figure 11 (opposite).

The performance of syringes can be improved by lubricating the seal inside on the edge of the plunger with a silicon lubricant obtainable from a plumber's shop. Please observe appropriate Health and Safety precautions if you do this.

Fastening

95 Hammer and nails

Nails have different shaped heads according to their purposes. The panel pin can be hit below

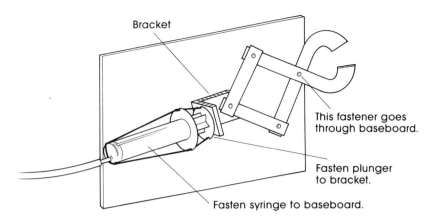

Bracket

This fastener goes through baseboard.

Fasten plunger to bracket.

Fasten syringe to baseboard.

Figure 11

the surface of the wood with minimum disfigurement. The roundhead nail can give extra gripping power while the clout nail secures soft material to wood. As they progress, children should be able to choose appropriate fastenings for particular purposes.

99–100   Making hinges 1 and 2

A variety of hinges are shown to reinforce the idea of choice. The simple Corriflute hinge is easy to make but less easy to attach, because the plastic is not easy to glue. The cotton cloth hinge used to be popular with model aeroplane builders. It takes glue well but is imprecise unless the cotton is used in strips of three as shown in Figure 12.

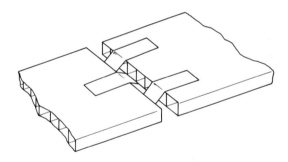

Figure 12

Bought-in hinges fastened securely will give the greatest strength.

Photography

101   A pinhole camera

The pinhole camera shown is just one version of the device. Even shoe boxes can be used but loading the photo-sensitive paper can be difficult. Beware of costs when starting this activity. Films can be quite expensive and some wastage is inevitable. Perhaps you need to

explore the shape and size of the box and the fastening it needs before the children have a go. Much depends on your aims in using a pinhole camera. Do you want to use it as a tool, or as a means of investigating the effect of light on photo-sensitive paper? *The Ilford Book of Photography* will be useful in this work.

Construction set

102–4   A home-made construction set

The dowel rod construction set has developed from an idea by Keith Geary, and has been used by many children from six years upwards. It offers a simple, cheap and very versatile resource for building structures. It is also highly durable. Young children accidentally damage paper art straws very easily; dowels are much more durable. Models can be built with it to test design ideas for structures as diverse as bridges, houses, disaster shelters, land yachts, windmills and car park barriers. It is invaluable as a tool for building prototype models as part of the design process. Many children find it easier to model in three dimensions than to try to explain ideas by drawing on paper. Using a construction set is a very good way of exploring and explaining possible solutions to a suitable problem. The modelling process (AT2 and AT3) can generate much discussion of ideas. As the model is changed to suit the flow of ideas, evaluation (AT4) follows on naturally. It has been found that working in pairs produces better results with the set. This is especially true with infants: one child holds the dowels while the other fastens the elastic band.

The strength of structures made with the set is heavily dependent on the creation of triangle shapes within the framework. The practice golfballs are not intended to be used to form a joint in the structure, as the strength of the joint would then solely be that of the ball. The plastic golfballs are intended to be used as wheels and pivots.

Another advantage of this set over other construction sets, is that the elastic band joint can be observed slowly giving way under test at particular pressure points. As the joint gives way it can be modified (AT4) so that a better structure evolves.

Very simple costing principles can be appreciated with the set if each dowel, ball and elastic band is given a cash value. Children can cost up their solutions to particular problems; the most effective structure would be the one which holds the most weight at the lowest cost.

Challenges for techniques for primary design and technology

These challenges are offered as another means of helping children solve problems and acquire a range of skills and knowledge that will increase their experience and develop their eventual design capability. They all relate to the techniques presented in this book. The Rainbow Technology Context Cards offer very open-ended challenges that allow considerable freedom of response. To teach skills and knowledge through such challenges is demanding, but highly rewarding. Such open-ended challenges can be interspersed with more focussed challenges such as those that demand a less broad range of experience and skill. The challenges given here can help develop the acquisition of skills and knowledge in controlled contexts. Given that partial solutions are shown in the Techniques sheets themselves, they may only need limited teacher intervention. Some of the challenges require the combination of techniques within a section.

You may choose to set up several of these challenges for different groups to attempt at the same time. Groups can then report back and demonstrate to each other what they have done. Within each section you will find challenges that use similar skills and knowledge, so that, if the group approach is used, the teacher can arrange for similar learning to occur for totally different end products.

When introducing a challenge to a group, the teacher needs to consider whether to lead into it through discussion or brainstorming and to be aware of children's needs. Do they need discussion time, planning time, and what resources do they require? It is important that children understand what is being asked of them. In order to overcome misunderstandings it is a good idea to display the challenge in large writing somewhere in the classroom and to leave it there for the duration of the activity.

Electricity

1 Make each type of switch or circuit to see how it works. (Bear in mind the need for progression. A child must understand the basic concepts of continuity in a circuit and the differences between insulators and conductors before attempting to make a switch.)

2 Make a model of a torch.

3 Put headlights on a buggy, model car, van or lorry.

4 Construct a flashing light for a lighthouse or on top of a car. Make it orange or blue in colour. Why should one of these colours be chosen?

5 Make some traffic lights.

6 Make a lamp post for a street, village or town environment. Does the choice of environment affect the design?

7 Put lighting into a doll's house.

8 Make a model of a room inside a cardboard box. Include both fixed and portable types of lighting.

9 Make a switch that works when a door is opened.

10 Make a switch to be operated by someone treading on a doormat.

11 Make a warning system that will automatically let you know if someone is outside a door of your house or classroom.

12 Make a remote control switch that will make a motor go backwards, forwards or stop.

13 Use an electric motor to turn a switch so that a light comes on all the time and a buzzer sounds intermittently, like the reversing system on big lorries or buses.

14 Make an educational toy to help the infant teacher teach about matching, e.g. matching colours to the words for their names. When the correct match is made a buzzer should sound.

15 Make an alarm so that if someone picks up the dinner money box a loud alarm should sound.

16 Make an alarm that can be fitted to a bicycle or favourite toy, so that if someone picks it up, a buzzer sounds.

17 Make a switch that works after a ten seconds delay, and then after three minutes delay.

18 Make a switch that can be made to work for a variety of different time delays. (Use the programmable disc idea but combine it with a motorised complex pulley system to reduce the speed.)

19 Make a game that relies on the careful steering of a ball bearing to score points.

20 Make an illuminated advertising sign where different groups of bulbs go on and off in sequence.

21 Make a weighing scale for a blind person.

22 Make a bendy wire skill tester.

Structures

1 Use the home-made construction set to make models of:

- a land yacht
- a bridge framework
- a car park barrier
- an aeroplane
- a house for the Three Little Pigs
- a lowering tool for the Supermarket Mice
- a tool for reaching things dropped from a wheel chair
- a light framework that can be simply covered to form a temporary shelter for people in a disaster area.

2 Construct a simple van model from paper. Strengthen this model by adding folded or rolled paper forms so that it will survive an impact.

3 Make a model dwelling, e.g. a house, caravan, tent, houseboat or narrow boat.

4 Make a small greenhouse in which to grow simple plants.

5 Make a box suitable for sending an Easter egg through the postal system.

6 Make a bird table.

7 Make a model fire engine.

8 Make a model of a system for cleaning windows on a tall block of flats.

9 Make a model of something to help you clean the upstairs windows on a house.

10 Make a simple weighing machine.

11 Devise an organisational structure to help plan and organise a school fair or a party.

12 Devise a system to help new pupils find their way around the school structure (buildings and organisational hierarchy).

13 Reorganise the classroom or school library.

14 Plan a quiet garden area for children who don't want to play football or run about the school playground.

Going round and round

1 Make a transporter for the Giant Jam Sandwich.

2 Put wheels on a box and use pushing as a source of energy to see how far it will go.

3 Make a lifting bridge, such as a drawbridge.

4 Make a faiground roundabout or ferris wheel model.

5 Make a simple crane.

6 Modify your simple crane design so that the system is geared down to make it easier to turn.

7 Make wheels for a gypsy caravan or a cart drawn by a horse.

8 Make a turning display stand in a shop window.

9 Use a pulley to lift a load.

10 Use two pulleys to make lifting the load easier.

11 Use four pulleys to make it really easy!

Making noises

1 Make a machine that will scare away mini-beasts.

2 Make a bird scarer that won't harm birds.

3 Make a clapping machine to save an audience from hurting their hands or becoming too tired.

4 Make a noisy machine to link to a door alarm switch.

5 Make musical instruments based on:

- shaking
- twanging
- banging
- rubbing.

6 Make a timing device that clacks when the time is up.

7 Make a machine which produces a noise by rotating something so that the noise is varied by altering the speed of rotation.

8 Make a machine that makes a noise that helps you feel happier.

9 Design and make a noise system for a quiz show to organise and control the teams.

10 Design and make a loud sound system for starting a race.

Motors

1 Use a balloon to propel a feather as far as possible across the classroom in a straight line. (Some very smooth string and a straw might help.)
2 Use a balloon to move a simple lightweight buggy.
3 Use a falling weight to turn a fairground ride.
4 Use an elastic band to develop a launcher for the fair testing of paper aeroplanes.
5 Make an elastic-powered model bus with simple passengers that jiggle about as it goes along. (Table tennis balls make good heads.)
6 Use a falling weight to move a vehicle more than one and a half metres.
7 Use the simple elastic motor to power a paddle steamer.

Releasing

1 Design and make a simple elastic band trigger for a paper aeroplane launcher.
2 Design and make a release system to create a fair test for buggies that are released down a slope to see how far they will roll.
3 Make a simple device to slow down the release of energy from the elastic band motor.
4 Make a simple brake for a turning shaft.
5 Make a telescopic stand and devise a hold and release system for setting the stand at different heights.

Making adjustments

1 Often the axle holes in cardboard box buggies wear bigger. Design a means of repairing or reducing the size of the holes.
2 Lever systems in models can be made to work differently by altering the position of a pivoted joint with respect to the fulcrum or pivot point. Design and make a system that can be used to experiment with levers and pivot points to try out different systems that may be needed in a model.
3 When making musical instruments from stretched cotton or elastic bands it is useful to be able to alter the tension. Suggest a means of doing this.
4 Plan a party, but beware that sometimes things go wrong, so include some means of changing the system quickly and easily.

5 Design a system for sorting different sized coins or marbles.
6 Operate a set of railway points or a signal from the far end of a table.
7 Make a sign for the home corner that says 'Open' or 'Closed', which can be operated from at least one metre away.
8 Design and make a system to open a drawer from at least two metres away.
9 Make a steerable vehicle that can be controlled from behind as you follow it.
10 Design a remote control system that will allow you to tip over a bucket when you are at least one metre away.

Mechanisms

1 Make a simple puppet with knee, hip, elbow and shoulder joints.
2 Make a robotic arm with syringes to provide movement.
3 Make a variety of pop-up greetings cards.
4 Make a pop-up story book.
5 Make moving models that can be fastened to a notice board and moved by pulling, pushing or turning.
6 Make a pull-along toy with an animal or person shape that moves as the toy moves along.
7 Make an advertising sign with an eye-catching movement in it.
8 Make a model of an Egyptian shaduf.
9 Make a hoist for a model car so that a mechanic can look beneath it during repair or servicing times.
10 Make a crossing barrier or a railway signal.

Pneumatics and hydraulics

1 Make a moving tongue for a dinosaur model.
2 Make an opening and closing jaw for a dinosaur wall display.
3 Make a lifting bridge.
4 Devise a safe method of tilting a chair forward to help an arthritic person get in and out.
5 Make a Jack-in-the-box.
6 Make a face with a hat that can be lifted off and on.
7 Use a syringe with a lever system to make a remote-controlled grab.
8 Set up a system to lift quite a heavy load with little effort.

Index of Applications

This index has been compiled to suggest ways in which you can use and combine the sheets to make particular models and artefacts. Its function is to serve as an ideas bank for possible solutions and as a stimulus to creative thinking. It is not intended to be exhaustive or prescriptive. Very often several different techniques will be given for the same requirement. Reference is made throughout to particular techniques that may be useful, and some general categories are also included where a large section of techniques all apply to one application. For example, nearly all of the section Going round and round is valuable for making vehicles. You may find it helpful also to refer to the Teacher's notes for particular techniques which will sometimes make clear why a particular technique is relevant to an application.

Advertising (see Signs)

Aeroplanes
jet propelled
70 Power from ballons
launching
71–3 Release and trigger mechanisms 1–3
launch pad frameworks
32–5 Frameworks for models 1–4; 102–4 A home-made construction set 1–3
modelling (for infants)
102–4 A home-made construction set 1–3

Alarms
2 Simple electrical components and materials 2 (reed switch); 8–9 Making electrical connections 1 and 2; 15–17 Switches that turn 1–3; 19 A pressure pad; 20–1 Membrane switches 1 and 2; 23–4 Tilt switches 1 and 2; 65 Making noises

Barriers (see Car park barriers)
Bell push (see Door bells)
Bird tables
38 An outdoor stand; 39 Stands with a round upright; 40 Adjustable stands

Boats
launching
71–4 Release and trigger mechanisms 1–4
mast and sails
102–4 A home-made construction set 1–3
motors for
67–70 Simple motors; all kinds of electric motors and switches
structures for
32–5 Frameworks for models 1–4; 41–3 Joining Corriflute 1–3; 44 Pivoting and hinging Corriflute; 102–4 A home-made construction set 1–3

Breakdown trucks
32–5 Frameworks for models 1–4; 61 Winches and winding; Going round and round

Bridges
30–1 Testing structures for strength 1 and 2, 32–5 Frameworks for models 1–4; 102–4 A home-made construction set 1–3
lifting
44 Pivoting and hinging Corriflute; 54 Pulleys and belts; 56 Gears; 61 Winches and winding; 92 Using a pneumatic or hydraulic system; 99–100 Making hinges 1 and 2; all kinds of switches and electric motors for powering a winch

Buggies (see Vehicles)
Buildings (see also Houses)
lifts in
3 Simple electrical components and materials 3 (microswitch); 54 Pulleys and belts; 56 Gears; 61 Winches and winding
structures for
32–5 Frameworks for models 1–4; 102–4 A home-made construction set 1–3
Burglar alarms (see Alarms)

Car park barriers
19 A pressure pad; 20–1 Membrane switches 1 and 2; 32–5 Frameworks for models 1–4; 44 Pivoting and hinging Corriflute; 54 Pulleys and belts; 56 Gears; 61 Winches and winding; 79 Remote control linkages; 87–8 Cams and eccentrics 1 and 2; 92 Using a pneumatic or hydraulic system; 99–100 Making hinges 1 and 2; 102–4 A home-made construction set 1–3
warning lights for (see Warning lights)
Cars (see Vehicles)
Castles
drawbridges for
54–60 Pulleys and gears; 61 Winches and winding; 99–100 Making hinges 1 and 2
structures for
41–3 Joining Corriflute 1–3; 44 Pivoting and hinging Corriflute
Circuit testers
4 Making circuits
Conveyor belts
32–5 Frameworks for models 1–4; 98 Fastening with everyday bits and pieces 3; Going round and round (pulleys and gears)
Cranes
32–5 Frameworks for models 1–4; 41–3 Joining Corriflute 1–3; 102–4 A home-made construction set 1–3; Going round and round (pulleys, gears, axles, wheels, tyres, winches); Mechanisms (levers, couplings); Electricity (motors, batteries, switches and lights)

Dinosaurs
27 Coloured lights; 92 Using pneumatic and hydraulic systems; 99–100 Making hinges 1 and 2; Electricity (switches)
Door bells
8–9 Making electrical connections 1 and 2; 11 Press switches; 15–17 Switches that turn 1–3; 19 A pressure pad; 27 Coloured lights (for deaf people)

Fairground mechanisms
Ferris wheels
32–5 Frameworks for models 1–4; 54 Pulleys and belts; 55 Pulleys and power; Going round and round (pulleys, winches, wheels, axles, gears)
lights in
18 A programmable switch; 27 Coloured lights
roundabouts
54 Pulleys and belts; 55 Pulleys and power; 61 Winches and winding; 62–3 Turntables 1 and 2; 64 Making turntables turn; 87–8 Cams and eccentrics 1 and 2
structures for
32–5 Frameworks for models 1–4; Going round and round; Pneumatics and hydraulics

Fire engines
15-17 Switches that turn 1-3; 27 Coloured lights; 32-5 Frameworks for models 1-4; 46-7 Rolling along 1 and 2; 49 Making wheels; 50 Tyres and treads; 52-3 Axles and spindles 1 and 2; 62-3 Turntables 1 and 2; 77-8 Adjustable ladders 1 and 2; 92 Using a pneumatic or hydraulic system; Motors

Fishing reels
61 Winches and winding; 75 One-way turning

Flashing lights
4 Making circuits; 10 Slide switches; 11 Press switches; 15-17 Switches that turn 1-3; 18 A programmable switch; 27 Coloured lights

Forklift trucks
32-5 Frameworks for models 1-4; 46 Rolling along 1; 49 Making wheels; 52-3 Axles and spindles 1 and 2; 54 Pulleys and belts; 55 Pulleys and power; 56 Gears; 61 Winches and winding; 92 Using a pneumatic or hydraulic system; all kinds of buzzers and alarms

Games
electrical
4 Making circuits (for circuit continuity for a bendy wire co-ordination game); *9 Making electrical connections 2* (for pinball, dexterity and matching games)
launching
74 Release and trigger mechanisms 4

Gates
32-5 Frameworks for models 1-4; 44 Pivoting and hinging Corriflute; 99-100 Making hinges 1 and 2; 102-4 A home-made construction set 1-3

Grabbers
83 Simple mechanisms 1; 93 Adjusting hydraulic systems

Greenhouses
32-5 Frameworks for models 1-4; 102-4 A home-made construction set 1-3

Houses
burglar alarms for (see Alarms)
doorbells for (see Doorbells)
lights in
10 Slide switches; 12 Reversing switches (see Teacher's Notes); *27 Coloured lights*
structures for
32-5 Frameworks for models 1-4; 102-4 A home-made construction set 1-3

Jack-in-the-box
65 Noise makers; 92 Using a pneumatic or hydraulic system; all kinds of buzzers and switches

Land yachts
32-5 Frameworks for models 1-4; 102-4 A home-made construction set

Laughter machines
65 Noise makers; 68-9 Power from a falling weight 1 and 2; 70 Power from balloons; 71-3 Release and trigger mechanisms 1-3; 80-2 Levers in models 1-3; 92 Using a pneumatic or hydraulic system; Going round and round

Lifts
3 Simple electrical components and materials 3 (microswitch); *32-5 Frameworks for models 1-4; 54 Pulleys and belts; 55 Pulleys and power; 56 Gears; 61 Winches and winding; 92 Using a pneumatic or hydraulic system;* Electricity (motors, batteries and switches)

Lighthouses
15-17 Switches that turn 1-3; 27 Coloured lights; 32-5 Frameworks for models 1-4; 62-3 Turntables 1 and 2

Mines and mining equipment (see also Lifts)
32-5 Frameworks for models 1-4; 54 Pulleys and belts; 55 Pulleys and power; 56 Gears; 67 Simple motors; 68-9 Power from falling weights 1 and 2; use of electric motors generally

Morse code buzzer
11 Press switches

Musical instruments
66 Noises from stretched fibres

Periscopes
32-5 Frameworks for models 1-4; 41-3 Joining Corriflute 1-3; 44 Pivoting and hinging Corriflute

Pop-up cards
80-2 Levers in models 1-3

Puppets
83 Simple mechanisms 1 (moving arms); *84 Simple mechanisms 2* (couplings); *99-100 Making hinges 1 and 2*

Railways
crossing barriers (see Car park barriers)
signals
20-1 Membrane switches 1 and 2; 27 Coloured lights; 79 Remote control linkages
turntables
62-3 Turntables 1 and 2; 64 Making turntables turn

Rain gauge (see Weather recording equipment)

Robots
4 Making circuits; 15-17 Switches that turn 1-3; 27 Coloured lights; 44 Pivoting and hinging Corriflute; 83 Simple mechanisms 1 (moving arms); *84-5 Simple mechanisms 2 and 3; 87-8 Cams and eccentrics 1 and 2*

Rockets
launching
71-4 Release and trigger mechanisms 1-4

Roundabouts (see Fairground mechanisms)

Sending messages
18 A programmable switch; 27 Coloured lights; 83-6 Simple mechanisms 1-4 (for semaphore systems); *92 Using a pneumatic or hydraulic system;* Electricity

Shop displays (see Signs)

Signs
10 Slide switches; 15-17 Switches that turn 1-3; 26 Connecting more than one light switch; 27 Coloured lights; 32-5 Frameworks for models 1-4; 62-3 Turntables 1 and 2; 65 Making noises; 99-100 Making hinges 1 and 2; Pneumatics and hydraulics

Stop switches
2 Simple electrical components 2 (reed switch); *3 Simple electrical components 3* (microswitch); *11 Press switches*

Theatres
32-5 Frameworks for models 1-4; 54 Pulleys and belts; 55 Pulleys and power (for curtains and stage effect); *83-6 Simple mechanisms 1-4; 92 Using a pneumatic or hydraulic system;* Electricity (lights and switches)

Timers
9 Making electrical connections 2 (ball-bearing connector); *24 Tilt switches 2* (pivot tilt switch); *71-4 Release and trigger mechanisms 1-4*

Torches
4 Making circuits; 27 Coloured lights; Electricity (switches)

Toys
65 Noise makers; 67 Simple motors; 68–9 Power from falling weights 1 and 2; 79 Remote control linkages; 80–2 Levers in models 1–3; 92 Using a pneumatic or hydraulic system; Electricity (especially lights and buzzers); Going round and round (for many kinds of wheeled vehicles)

Traffic lights
18 A programmable switch; 19 A pressure pad; 25 Light sources from a battery; 26 Connecting more than one light source; 27 Coloured lights

Trains (see Railway and Vehicles)

Vehicles
lights on
25 Light sources using a battery; 27 Coloured lights
motors for
46–7 Rolling along 1 and 2; 67 Simple motors; 68–9 Power from a falling weight 1 and 2; 70 Power from balloons; use of electric motors generally
obstacle detectors on

3 Simple electrical components and materials 3 (microswitch)
structures for
32–5 Frameworks for models 1–4; 36–7 Frameworks from shadows 1 and 2; 46–7 Rolling along 1 and 2
wheels for
46–7 Rolling along 1 and 2; 48 Wheels from plywood discs; 49 Making wheels; 50 Tyres and treads; 51 Wheels for different conditions; 52–3 Axles and spindles 1 and 2

Warning lights (see Flashing lights)

Washing machines
28 Logic circuits; 41–3 Joining Corriflute 1–3; Switches (programmable switch, reed switches and microswitches); Going round and round

Weather recording equipment
rain gauges
3 Simple electrical components and materials 3 (microswitch); *23–4 Tilt switches 1 and 2*

Windmills
32–5 Frameworks for models 1–4; 52–3 Axles and spindles 1 and 2; 54 Pulleys and belts; 55 Pulleys and power; 56 Gears; 61 Winches and winding; Going round and round (wheels)

Simple electrical components and materials 1

There are many inexpensive electrical components which will help with easy circuit making. Remember that continuity is essential and relies on metal to metal contact. The following is a selection of components that you may find useful in electrical work.

Crocodile clips offer a quick way of making electrical contacts. Uninsulated clips can cause short circuits but they do show how the clip works with a spring keeping the jaws together.

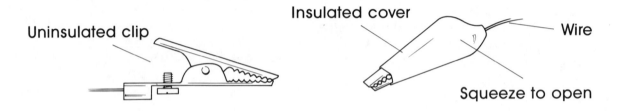

Paper clips are useful for making quick connections.

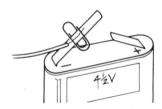

Rolls of self-adhesive copper strip are useful for gluing to materials to make electrical contacts. The strip is about 6 mm wide.

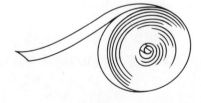

Aluminium cooking foil can be stuck on to card or hardboard to make contact surfaces.

2 Electricity

Simple electrical components and materials 2

Two-amp terminal block is a nylon moulding containing brass connectors that will hold wires tight under screws. It is invaluable for joining wires and components. The terminal block can easily be divided up with scissors or a sharp knife.

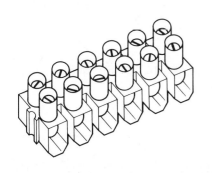

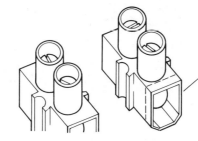

Use scissors or a sharp knife to cut bits off the end.

Sharp knives are dangerous.

Here are some ways in which the terminal block is useful for connecting components:

Use hot glue gun to fix blocks to a motor.

Use hot glue gun to fix switch and blocks to lolly stick.

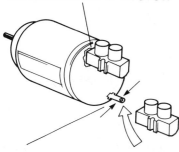

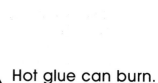

Reed switch

Crimp tag with pliers in order to fit in terminal block.

Slide the block on to the connecting tag and tighten the screw. Some plastic may need to be trimmed from the block.

Hot glue can burn.

A reed switch is a switch that can be operated by a magnet. It is useful for situations where it is necessary to have a gap between the switch and the method of operating.

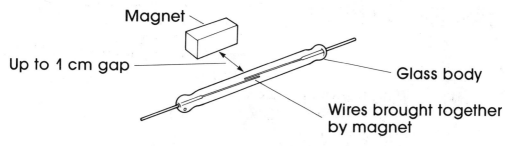

Magnet

Up to 1 cm gap

Glass body

Wires brought together by magnet

Simple electrical components and materials 3

A microswitch is a useful switch which needs only a light pressure to make it work.

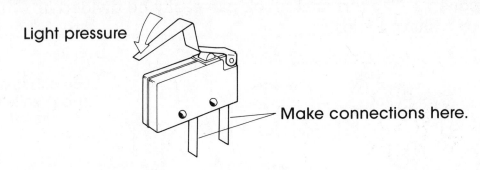

Light pressure

Make connections here.

Light-emitting diodes (LEDs) are delicate bulbs useful in model making. They are available in red, green and amber. A reflector that clips on to an LED helps to focus the light more strongly.

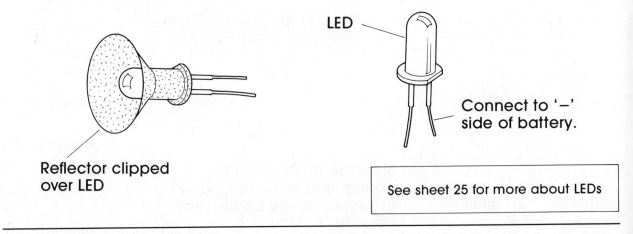

LED

Connect to '–' side of battery.

Reflector clipped over LED

See sheet 25 for more about LEDs

A hand drill is useful for tidying up trailing pairs of wires. The wires can be neatly twisted together.

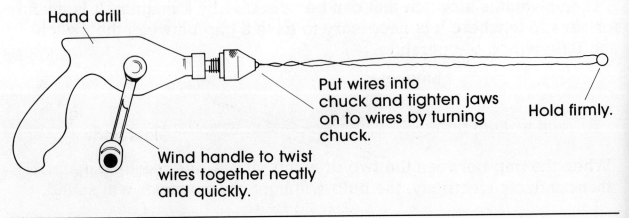

Hand drill

Put wires into chuck and tighten jaws on to wires by turning chuck.

Hold firmly.

Wind handle to twist wires together neatly and quickly.

Making circuits

The ideas of insulation, conduction and continuity are absolutely vital. They need to be clearly understood.

Conduction

Most electrical wire is covered by plastic insulation. The wire must be bare to make a good electrical contact.

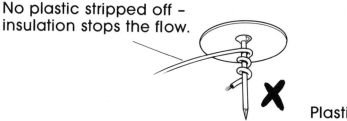

No plastic stripped off – insulation stops the flow.

Plastic stripped off – conduction can happen.

Continuity

To make a circuit the electricity must go from one side of the battery, through a bulb or motor and back to the other side of the battery.

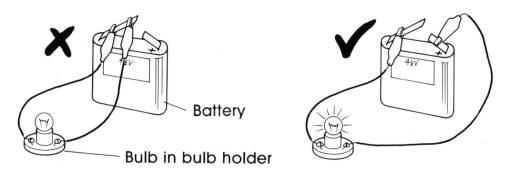

Battery

Bulb in bulb holder

A simple continuity or circuit tester

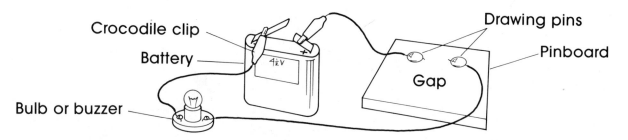

Crocodile clip

Drawing pins

Battery

Pinboard

Gap

Bulb or buzzer

When the gap between the two drawing pins is bridged by a material that conducts electricity, the bulb will light or the buzzer will sound.

5 Electricity

Common problems with bulbs, batteries and circuits

Match the bulb to the battery

It is important to choose an appropriate bulb for the battery being used. The bulb voltage needs to be the same as or bigger than the battery voltage.

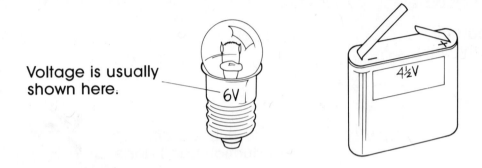

Voltage is usually shown here.

6V

4½V

If you use batteries in a holder, add the voltages of the individual batteries to give their combined voltage.

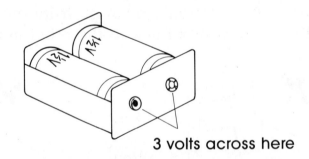

3 volts across here

Never connect the two terminals of a battery together without a bulb or something else in the circuit. (This is especially true of rechargable cells.) This would drain the battery very quickly and even cause harm to the person doing it.

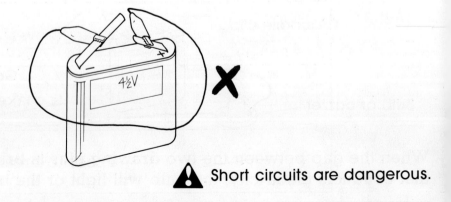

4½V

Short circuits are dangerous.

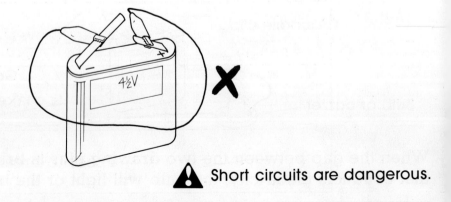

Electricity

Symbols for electrical circuits

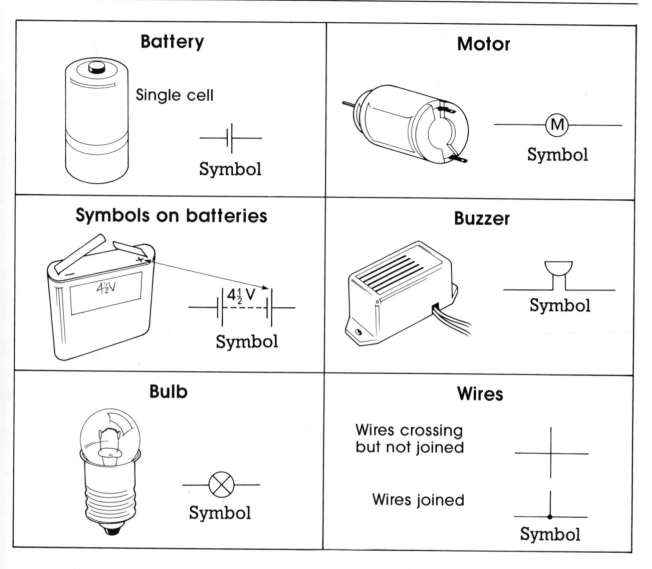

Battery	Motor
Single cell	
Symbol	Symbol
Symbols on batteries	**Buzzer**
$4\frac{1}{2}$V	
Symbol	Symbol
Bulb	**Wires**
Symbol	Wires crossing but not joined / Wires joined / Symbol

Switch symbols	
	On-off
	Change-over
	Press-to-make
	Press-to-break

Using symbols for electrical circuits

The simple lighting circuit on sheet 10

The circuit uses a bulb, a battery and a home-made switch.

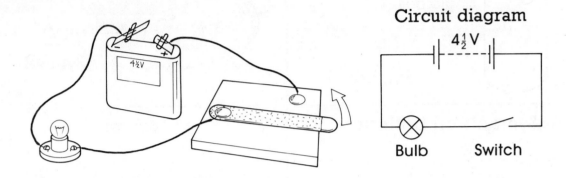

Circuit diagram

$4\frac{1}{2}$ V

Bulb   Switch

The change-over lighting circuit on sheet 10

The circuit uses two bulbs, a battery and a home-made switch.

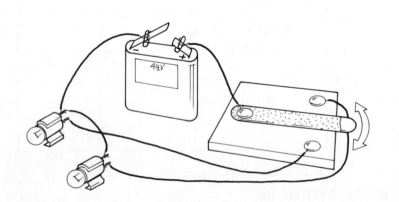

Circuit diagram

Wires joined (look at the bulb connections)

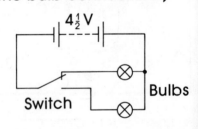

$4\frac{1}{2}$ V

Switch   Bulbs

The press-to-make switch on sheet 11 used as a Morse code buzzer

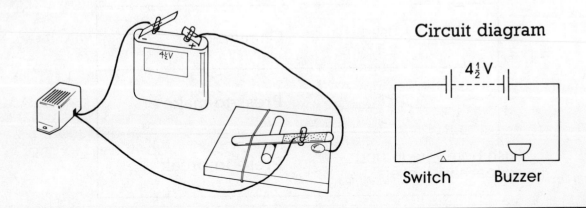

Circuit diagram

$4\frac{1}{2}$ V

Switch   Buzzer

Making electrical connections 1

You can make a useful circuit board by splitting up a 2-amp terminal block. Glue the single pieces on to hardboard, thick card or Corriflute. These small boards can be fitted inside models quite easily.

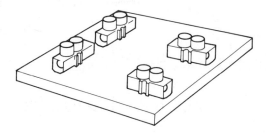

Circuit board springs are another easy way to make up simple circuits.

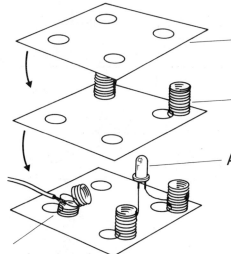

Card or Corriflute
Holes made with a desk-type paper punch, leather punch or Maun paper drill

Push in springs and slide sideways.

Attach an LED (light-emitting diode) like this.

Bend spring back
and insert bare wire like this.

Push-on spade connectors are useful.

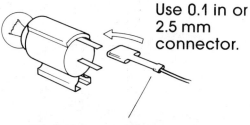

Use 0.1 in or
2.5 mm
connector.

Push bare wire in and
squeeze with pliers.

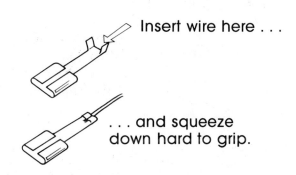

Insert wire here . . .

. . . and squeeze
down hard to grip.

Making electrical connections 2

Connections without solder

1

Small screwdriver

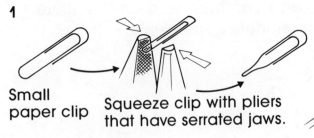

Small paper clip

Squeeze clip with pliers that have serrated jaws.

Push insulated wire and the clip into 2-amp terminal block and tighten screws.

2 The paper clip connector can be used in various ways.

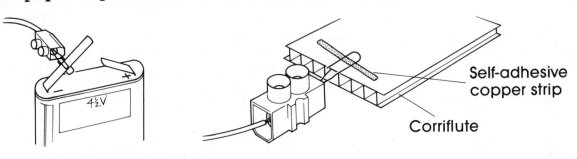

4½V

Self-adhesive copper strip

Corriflute

A ball-bearing connector

When the ball falls into the hole the tracks are connected.

Ball bearing

Glue cards together.

Thick card

Pair of copper strips

Gap of 2 mm

Hidden connections

Contact is made by touching each end of Strip 1 through the holes.

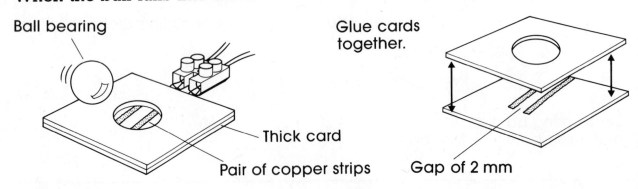

Aluminium foil (Strip 1) stuck down with double-sided tape

Insulating tape where two strips cross

4½V

Electricity

Slide switches

A simple on-off slide switch

1

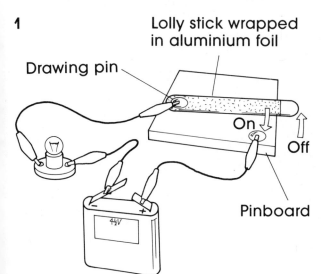

Lolly stick wrapped in aluminium foil

Drawing pin

On

Off

Pinboard

2 Drawing pins

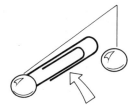

Move clip to control electricity.

Loop bare wire under pin.

3

Either make a hole with a paper punch or Maun paper drill . . .

Lolly stick

. . . or glue card to lolly stick and make the hole in the card.

Wrap lolly stick in aluminium foil.

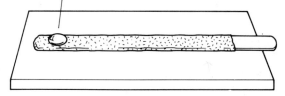

Pin lolly stick to soft board or Sundeala.

A change-over switch

The elastic band improves the quality of the electrical contact.

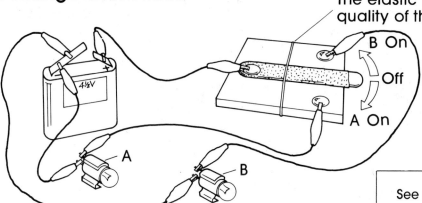

B On

Off

A On

A

B

See sheet 7 for circuit diagram

Press switches

A press-to-make switch for a bulb or buzzer

Elastic band keeps contacts apart until switch is pressed.

Drawing pins

Dowel rod

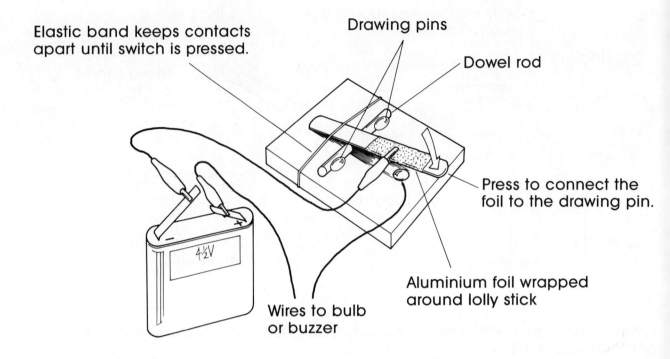

Press to connect the foil to the drawing pin.

4½V

Wires to bulb or buzzer

Aluminium foil wrapped around lolly stick

See sheet 7 for circuit diagram

A press-to-break switch for a bulb or buzzer

Wires to battery and bulb or buzzer

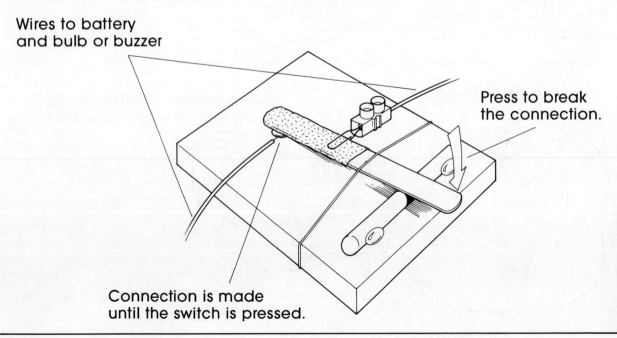

Press to break the connection.

Connection is made until the switch is pressed.

Reversing switches

A sliding switch to reverse a motor

1

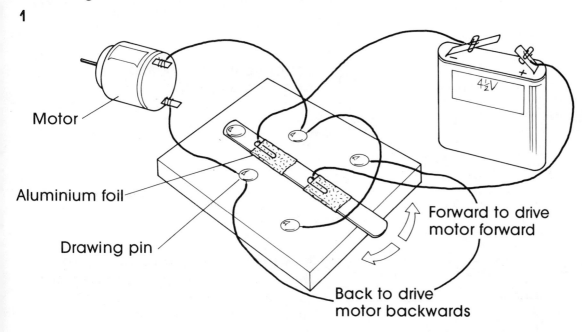

Motor

Aluminium foil

Drawing pin

Forward to drive
motor forward

Back to drive
motor backwards

$4\frac{1}{2}V$

See sheet 10 for slide switch

2 This shows how the flow of electricity from the battery through the motor can be reversed using the switch. As drawn, the '+' side of the battery is connected to C. When the switch is moved forward, the '−' side is connected to C.

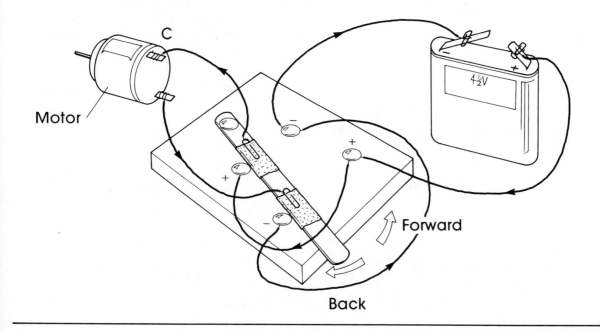

C

Motor

$4\frac{1}{2}V$

Forward

Back

Making switches from everyday items 1

A press-to-break peg switch

1

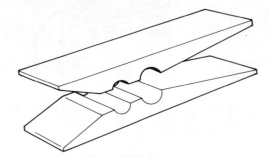

Separate the two halves of a clothes peg.

2

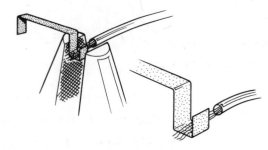

Bend a narrow strip (3 mm wide) of thin metal to fit around the peg. Use 'Atomic strip' draught excluder or similar thin sheet metal.

Bare some stranded wire and attach it to the metal by squeezing hard with pliers.

3

Sticky tape

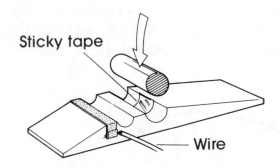

Wire

Use double-sided sticky tape to fasten a piece of dowel rod to one half of the peg.

Attach metal with double-sided sticky tape. This piece of metal makes one contact. Attach metal to the other half of the peg to make the second contact.

4 This is a normally-closed (NC) switch.

Elastic band

Put the two halves of the peg switch together.

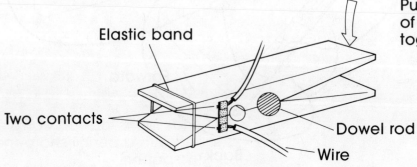

Two contacts

Dowel rod

Wire

Making switches from everyday items 2

A press-to-make peg switch

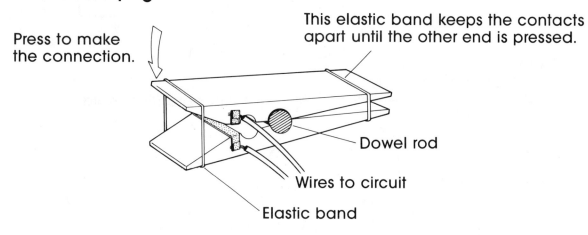

Press to make the connection.

This elastic band keeps the contacts apart until the other end is pressed.

Dowel rod

Wires to circuit

Elastic band

This is a normally-open (NO) switch.

A latch

1 Sometimes it is useful to make a normally-open switch stay on with a latch.

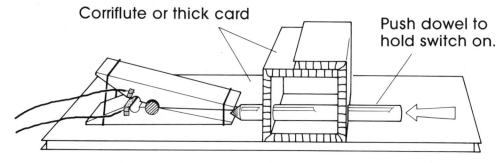

Corriflute or thick card

Push dowel to hold switch on.

Glue peg and Corriflute frame to base.

2 A similar latch could be made for a normally-closed switch.

Push dowel to hold switch open.

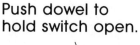

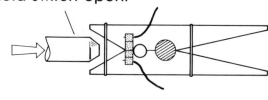

The ends of the dowels can be shaped with a pencil sharpener, rasp or glasspaper.

Switches that turn 1

1 Drawing pins about
3 mm apart with bared wire
trapped underneath

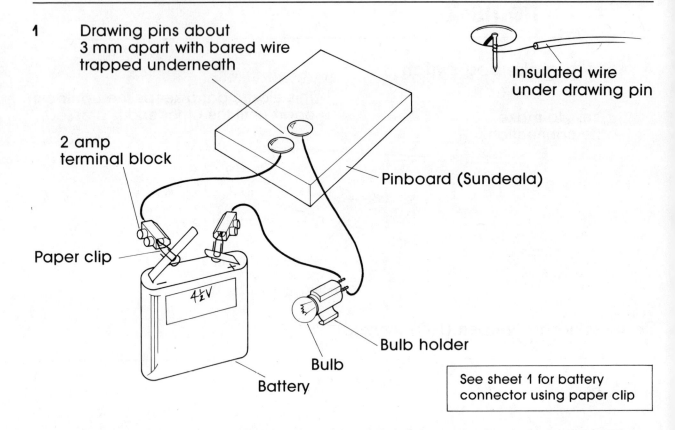

Insulated wire
under drawing pin

2 amp
terminal block

Paper clip

$4\frac{1}{2}$V

Pinboard (Sundeala)

Bulb holder

Bulb

Battery

See sheet 1 for battery
connector using paper clip

2 Thick card disc diameter 10 cm

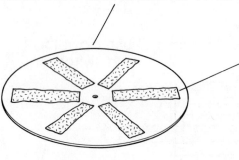

Aluminium cooking foil strips about half
a centimetre wide stuck on with Pritt
Stick or similar glue

Turn card disc upside down and pin to
pinboard base so that one of the
aluminium strips is on top of both
drawing pin heads.

3 Drawing
pin

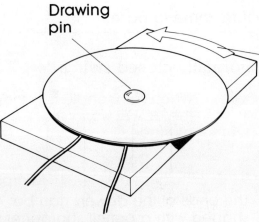

Use your thumb to turn the card disc
around. As the foil strips go over the
drawing pins the bulb should light.

Wires to bulb and battery

16

Switches that turn 2

A magnetic switch

1 This switch works by operating a reed switch. When the handle is turned the magnet comes round and works the switch.

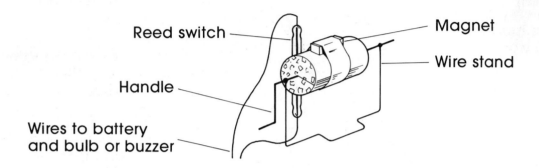

Reed switch — Magnet

— Wire stand

Handle —

Wires to battery
and bulb or buzzer

2 To make the switch:

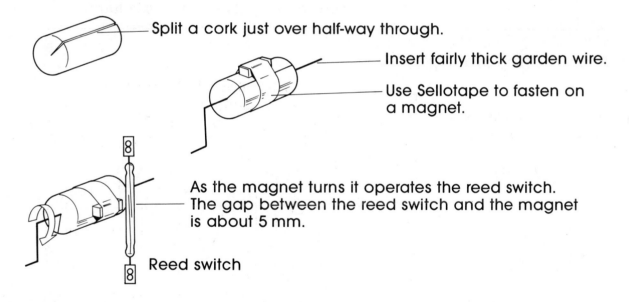

— Split a cork just over half-way through.

— Insert fairly thick garden wire.

— Use Sellotape to fasten on a magnet.

As the magnet turns it operates the reed switch. The gap between the reed switch and the magnet is about 5 mm.

Reed switch

A turning switch for a microswitch

A microswitch is
operated by
a plunger.

Tape dowel to the cork
instead of a magnet.
Mount as before.

When the handle is turned
the dowel works the
plunger.

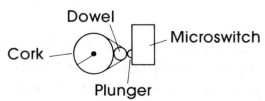

Dowel

Microswitch

Cork —

Plunger

Switches that turn 3

A lolly stick rotating switch

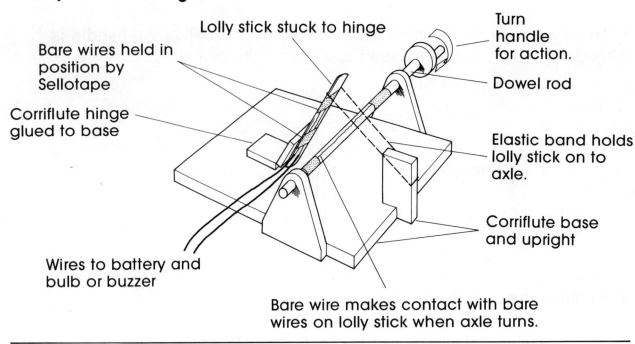

Lolly stick stuck to hinge

Bare wires held in position by Sellotape

Corriflute hinge glued to base

Turn handle for action.

Dowel rod

Elastic band holds lolly stick on to axle.

Corriflute base and upright

Wires to battery and bulb or buzzer

Bare wire makes contact with bare wires on lolly stick when axle turns.

A card disc rotating switch

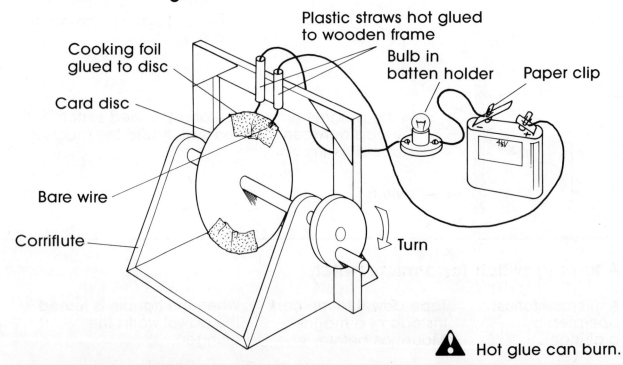

Plastic straws hot glued to wooden frame

Cooking foil glued to disc

Card disc

Bulb in batten holder

Paper clip

Bare wire

Corriflute

Turn

⚠ Hot glue can burn.

As the disc rotates, the foil connects the two bare wires. These wires need a supporting framework, one form of which is shown. Other methods are worth exploring.

Electricity

A programmable switch

A card disc and cooking foil switch can have several contacts on it to carry out a sequence of switching instructions. This sort of switch is a very simple model of an automatic washing machine controller.

1

Each pair of wires completes a circuit. You can have more than the two pairs shown. The wires can go to bulbs, buzzers and LEDs (light-emitting diodes). Use stranded wire.

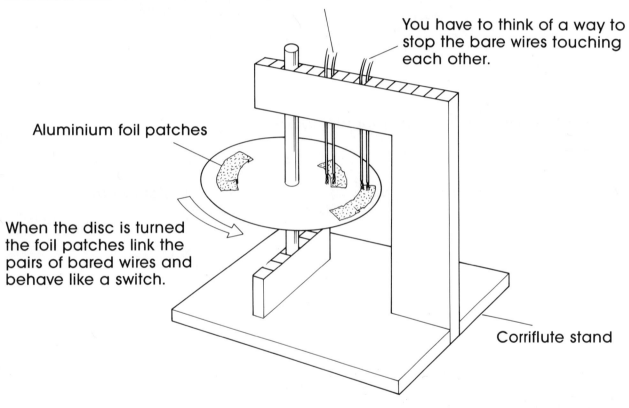

You have to think of a way to stop the bare wires touching each other.

Aluminium foil patches

When the disc is turned the foil patches link the pairs of bared wires and behave like a switch.

Corriflute stand

2

By gluing the foil patches in chosen places you can create as many sequences as you like.

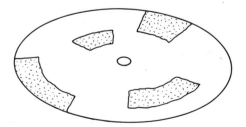

A pressure pad

1 Make two contacts of foil and card.

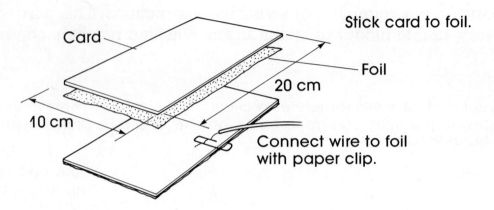

Card

Stick card to foil.

Foil

20 cm

10 cm

Connect wire to foil with paper clip.

2 Cut a hole in a piece of fire retardant foam.

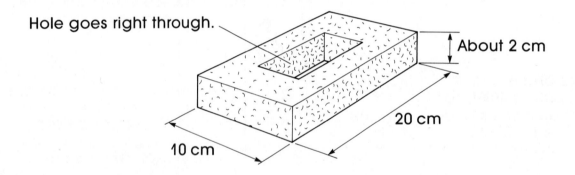

Hole goes right through.

About 2 cm

20 cm

10 cm

3 Glue the contacts to the top and bottom of the foam with the foil surfaces inwards. When the pad is pressed, the bulb lights.

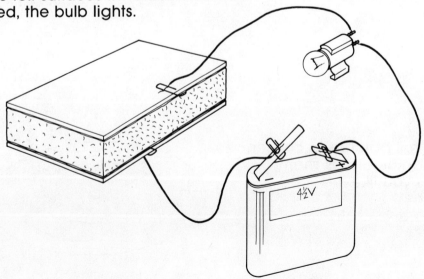

4½V

Electricity

Membrane switches 1

Making a membrane switch

1 The switch has two layers of cooking foil or foil-backed paper. They are separated by card with a hole in it. When the top layer is pressed, it connects to the bottom layer and works like a switch.

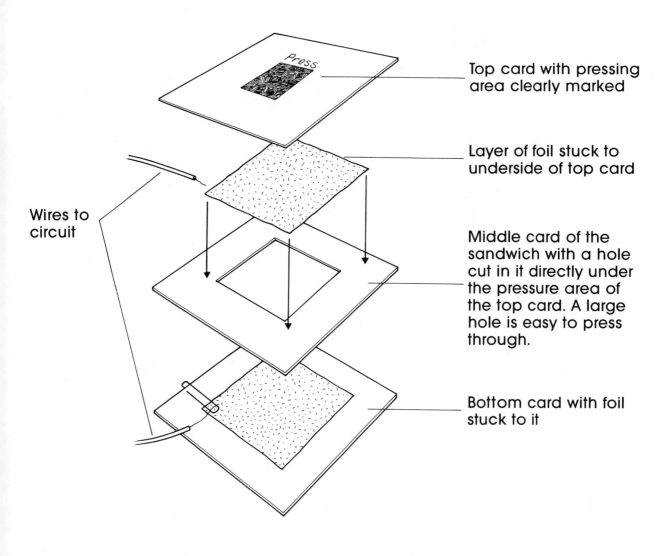

Top card with pressing area clearly marked

Layer of foil stuck to underside of top card

Wires to circuit

Middle card of the sandwich with a hole cut in it directly under the pressure area of the top card. A large hole is easy to press through.

Bottom card with foil stuck to it

Continued

Membrane switches 2

2 Before sticking the layers together you need to make the electrical connections to the top and bottom layers of the sandwich.

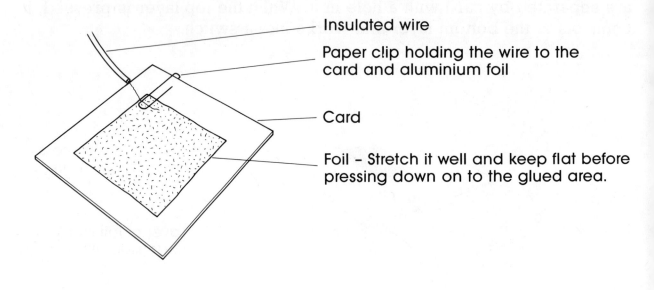

Insulated wire

Paper clip holding the wire to the card and aluminium foil

Card

Foil – Stretch it well and keep flat before pressing down on to the glued area.

Another membrane switch

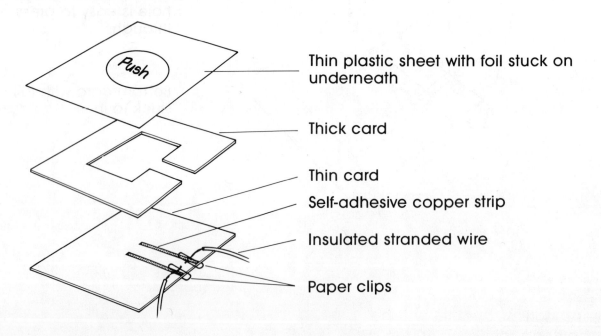

Push

Thin plastic sheet with foil stuck on underneath

Thick card

Thin card

Self-adhesive copper strip

Insulated stranded wire

Paper clips

Membrane switches 3

A multi-way membrane panel

This panel allows a different electrical item to work for each button pressed, for example, a bulb, buzzer or motor.

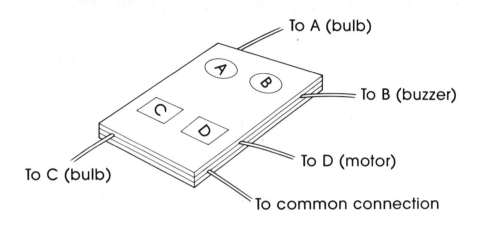

To A (bulb)

To B (buzzer)

To D (motor)

To common connection

To C (bulb)

To make the panel:

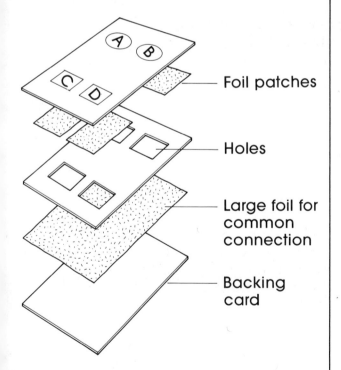

Foil patches

Holes

Large foil for common connection

Backing card

Each patch A, B, C, D will be connected independently to the common connection by pressing. Glue all the layers together.

The circuit diagram looks like this:

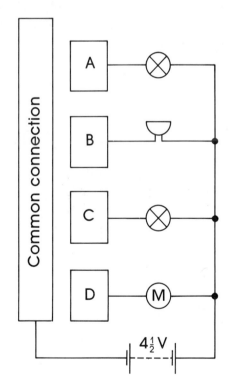

Tilt switches 1

Tilt switches sense movement of a rocking type. If a bicycle was left leaning against a wall and moved without permission, then the switch would operate and sound an alarm.

A tilt switch made from a 35 mm film cassette case

1 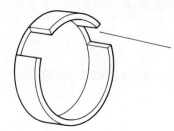   Cut two notches in the cap of the cassette case.

2 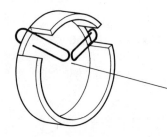   Attach two paper clips so that the ends are nearly touching.

3 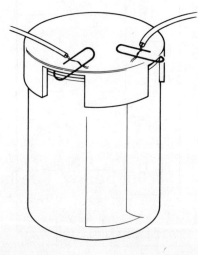   Wires to circuit

Replace lid on cassette case after putting a fairly big ball bearing inside. If you cannot find a ball bearing try wrapping a marble in aluminium foil.

When the cassette is tilted, the ball bearing will roll down and complete the circuit.

Tilt switches 2

A matchbox tilt switch

Make the aluminium foil contacts as shown. Put a steel ball-bearing with 12 mm or 15 mm diameter inside the matchbox. Tilt the box and the ball should touch the two foil contacts.

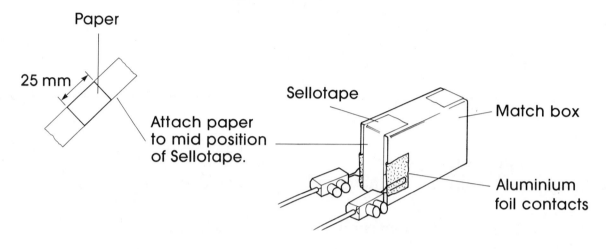

A pivot tilt switch

1 When the ball rolls between the foil, contact is made.

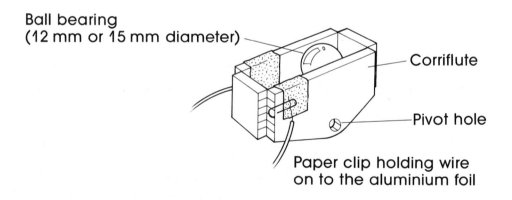

2 Try suspending the tilt switch from above and from below. See how much the sensitivity changes.

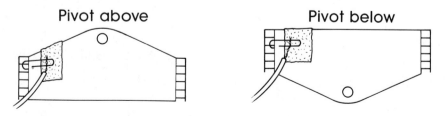

Electricity

Light sources using a battery

Bulbs

A torch bulb has a filament. This glows very brightly because the electricity has made it very hot.

White heat

LEDs

LEDs are light-emitting diodes. They have coloured plastic tops that are red, green or amber. They have to be connected very carefully.

1

The light is brighter if viewed from the end.

Flat surface on side of the LED

Legs of different lengths

2 You have to connect the LED to the battery carefully, using a resistor.

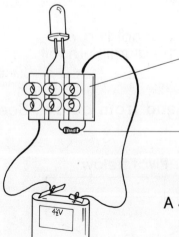

Use terminal block to connect the LED and resistor to the battery.

The resistor protects the LED which can only cope with small amounts of current.

A $4\frac{1}{2}$ volt battery needs a resistor of 150 ohms.

Connecting more than one light source

Bulbs

1

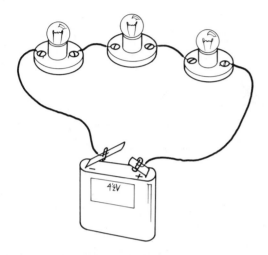

Here each bulb is connected to the next bulb in turn. This is known as a series connection. Try it and see how brightly the bulbs glow.

2

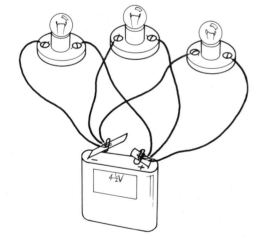

Here each bulb is connected directly to the battery. This is a parallel connection. Compare the brightness with that of the series connection.

LEDs

If more than three LEDs (light-emitting diodes) are connected together a resistor may not be needed, but be careful. LEDs can get hot enough to melt.

For a $4\frac{1}{2}$ volt battery, a resistor will not be needed if you have more than three LEDs.

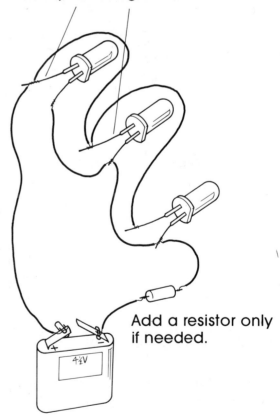

Legs of similar length are joined together.

Add a resistor only if needed.

Coloured lights

LEDs

LEDs (light-emitting diodes) are good for lighting Lego models. They fit exactly into Lego Technic blocks.

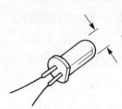

LED has a diameter of 5 mm.

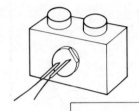

See sheet 25 for wiring information

Bulbs

1 Plastic foils or thin sheets of coloured film can make good coloured effects. Take care not to get the foil too close to the bulb.

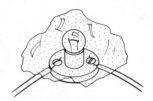

2 Different coloured plastics can be stuck behind holes in card to make traffic lights.

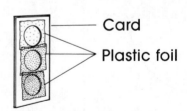

Card

Plastic foil

3 Foil lining of tubes with the bulb inside can make an interesting effect.

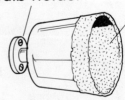

Batten type bulb holder

Various yoghurt pots or other pudding containers can make good reflectors when lined with foil.

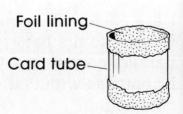

Foil lining

Card tube

Electricity

Logic circuits

In some automatic machines it is necessary to arrange a sequence of events. Electric logic can be used to do this. Here are logic circuits that use AND and OR systems.

AND systems

The bulb only lights if switches A and B are both pressed.

As many switches as you want can be connected, provided you connect them in series as shown.

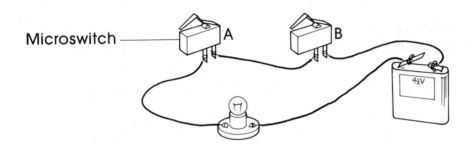

OR systems

Now the bulb lights if either switch A or switch B is pressed.

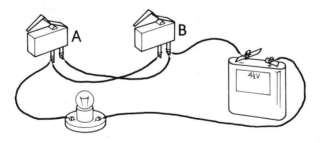

OR and AND systems

OR and AND systems can be combined.

In this system the bulb lights if you press C and (B or A).

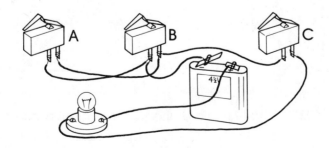

Making structures with the home-made construction set

All these structures or frameworks rely on the strength and rigidity of the triangle shape.

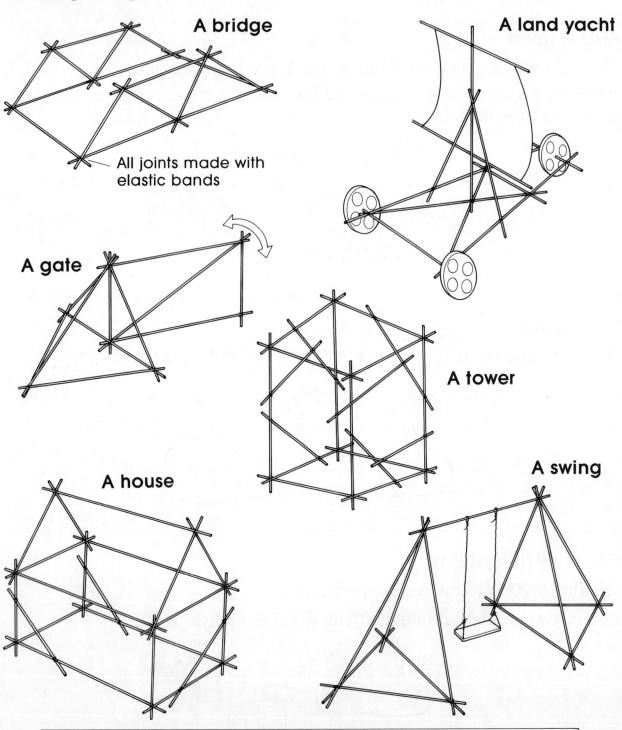

A bridge

All joints made with elastic bands

A land yacht

A gate

A tower

A house

A swing

See sheets 102, 103 and 104 for information on the home-made construction set

Testing structures for strength 1

1 You can test paper structures for strength like this:

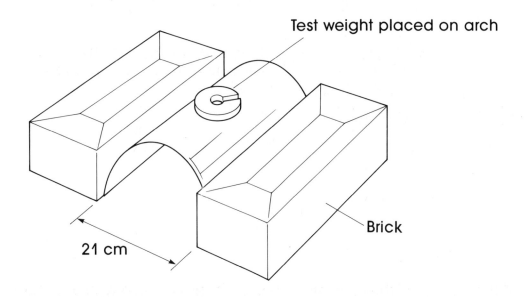

Test weight placed on arch

21 cm

Brick

2 Make and test these bridges:

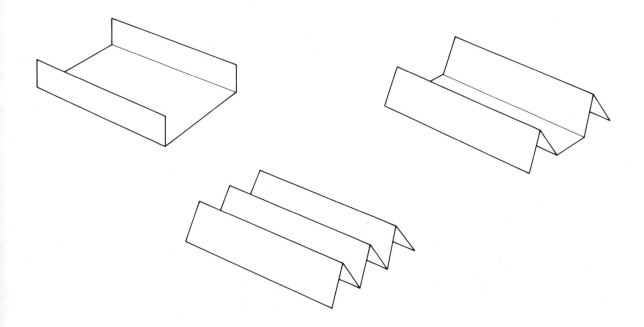

Each bridge is made from a single sheet of A4 paper without glue or Sellotape.

What other bridge shapes can you make and test?

Testing structures for strength 2

1 You can test tube structures like this:

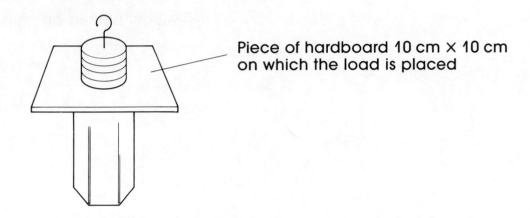

Piece of hardboard 10 cm × 10 cm
on which the load is placed

2 Make and test these tubes. Use a sheet of A4 paper for each one. Join the sides with Sellotape.

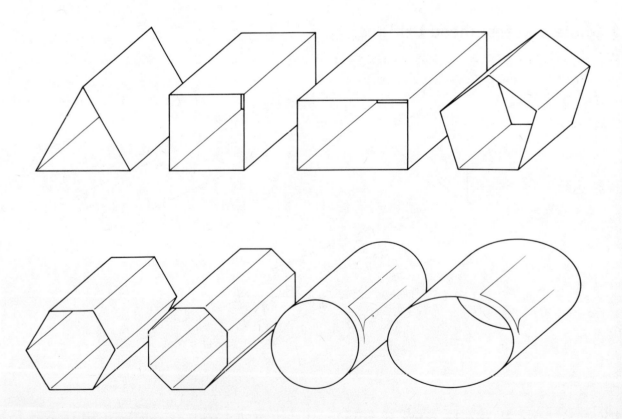

Which tube is the strongest?

Is your test fair?

Structures

Frameworks for models 1

1 Houses and other buildings have their roofs made with trusses, such as this one. The long lengths of wood are joined by nailing on pieces of plywood. The nails go right through and are hammered or clenched.

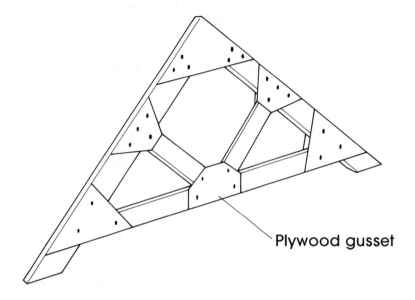

Plywood gusset

2 It is easy to make strong models by using the ideas in the roof truss. By sticking a card triangle either side of two pieces of stripwood a strong structure can be built.

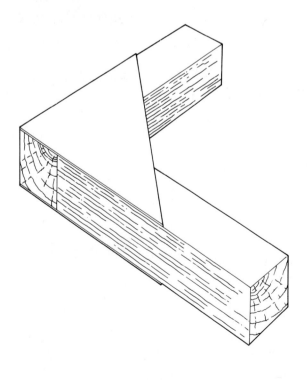

Continued

Frameworks for models 2

3 To make a framework you will need several pieces of wood of the same thickness.

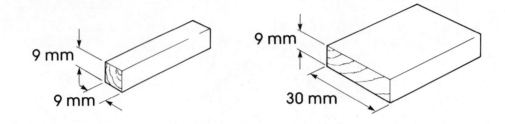

Useful sizes are: 9 mm × 9 mm, 10 mm × 10 mm, 12 mm × 12 mm, 9 mm × 20 mm, 12 mm × 20 mm, 9 mm × 30 mm or 12 mm × 30 mm.

4 You will need lots of triangles cut from thin card.

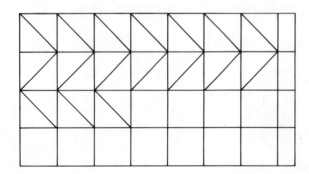

Mark out many squares 3 cm × 3 cm or many squares using the width of the ruler.

Put in the diagonals.

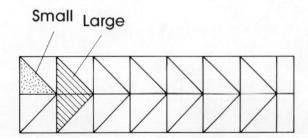

Cut out small and large triangles.

Continued

Frameworks for models 3

5 Cut wood strips to the length you need.

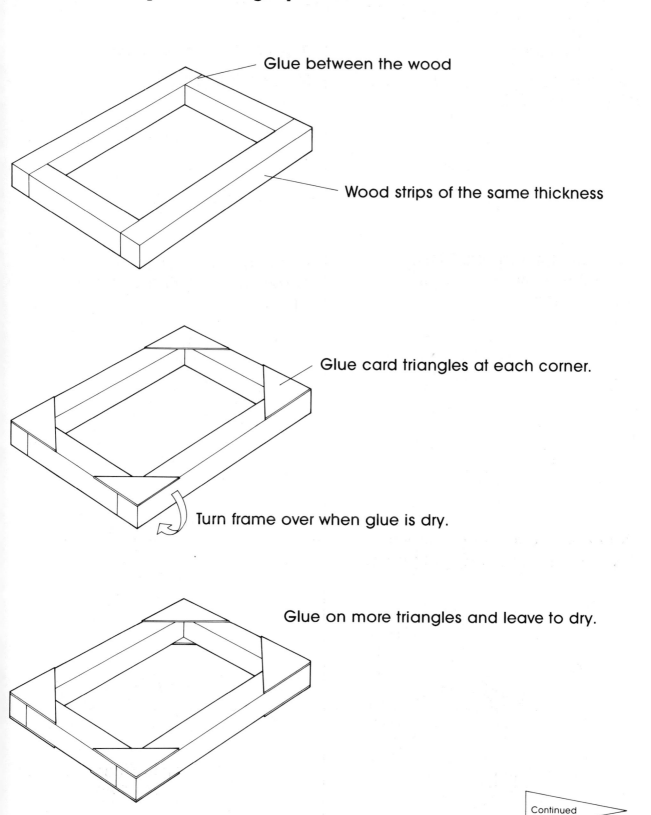

Glue between the wood

Wood strips of the same thickness

Glue card triangles at each corner.

Turn frame over when glue is dry.

Glue on more triangles and leave to dry.

Continued

Frameworks for models 4

Now you have made one simple framework, you will need to enlarge it to make a complete structure.

6 A box-like structure

Make another framework exactly like the first one.

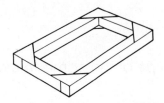

Cut out and fold eight large triangles. Glue on to both frameworks.

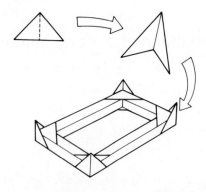

Join both frameworks together by using short lengths of wood.

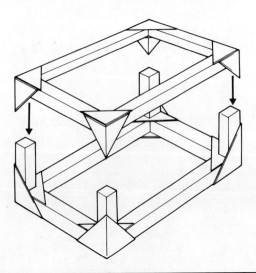

7 A roof-like structure

Make a framework.

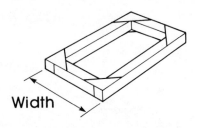

Width

Cut two pieces of wood to fit across the end of the frame.

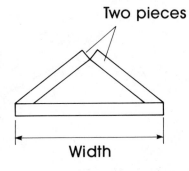

Two pieces

Width

Cut out from a large triangle

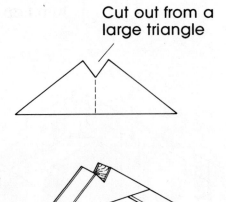

Fit two card triangles to the frame.

Frameworks from shadows 1

1 An easy way of making a framework is to draw the shadow of what you want to build on to some card.

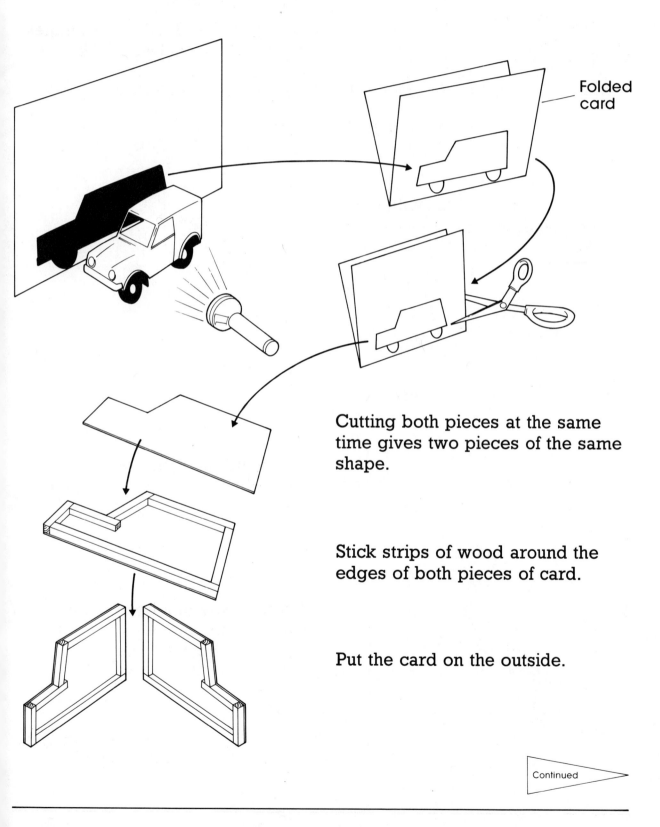

Folded card

Cutting both pieces at the same time gives two pieces of the same shape.

Stick strips of wood around the edges of both pieces of card.

Put the card on the outside.

Continued

Frameworks from shadows 2

2

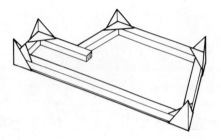

Stick small triangles on to increase strength.

Glue on the folded large triangles to join the two halves of the model together.

Join the two halves with further strips of wood.

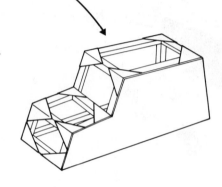

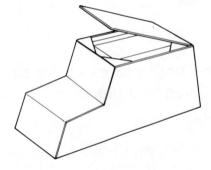

You could glue card on all the way round.

3

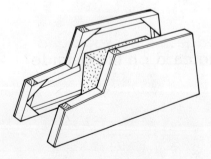

Another way of joining the two halves of the model is to fix a small box between them.

An outdoor stand

1

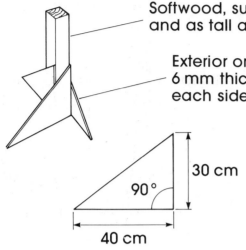

Softwood, such as pine, about 45 mm square and as tall as needed, up to about 1 m or 1.5 m

Exterior or marine grade plywood triangles about 6 mm thick and shaped to be a good fit. Fix one to each side of the upright.

The triangles need to be roughly the shape shown.

Use galvanised nails.

30 cm

90°

40 cm

2 Cut four triangles to your chosen size and shape.

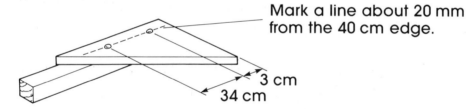

Mark a line about 20 mm from the 40 cm edge.

3 cm

34 cm

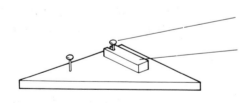

Mark nail positions and select a nail with a large head.

Use one of the nail holders and start the nail into the plywood at both positions.

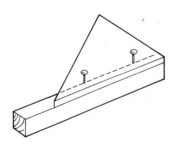

Line up the edges of the wood and hammer the nails in.

Repeat for the other triangles.

See sheet 95 for nail holder

Stands with a round upright

Plastic or steel tube. Steel should be protected from the weather by painting.

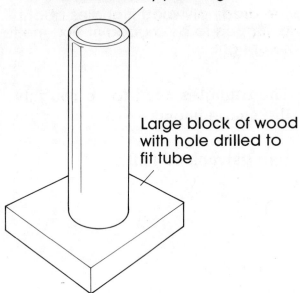

Large block of wood with hole drilled to fit tube

Bent wire hooks

String

Pour in sand and gravel.

At least 30 cm depth

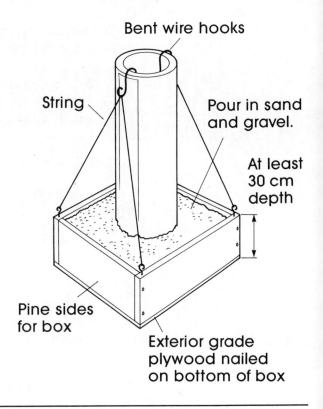

Pine sides for box

Exterior grade plywood nailed on bottom of box

Plywood this side not shown for clarity (dotted outline only).

Plywood is slotted to fit over base.

Frame made of softwood about 45 mm × 15 mm

Use galvanised nails and wood preservative or oil-based paint.

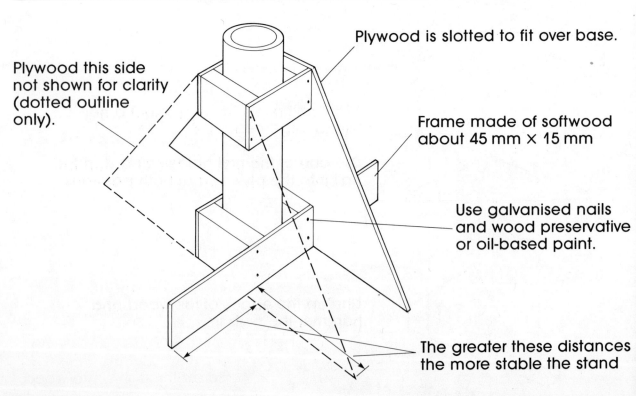

The greater these distances the more stable the stand

See sheet 95 for use of hammer and nails

Adjustable stands

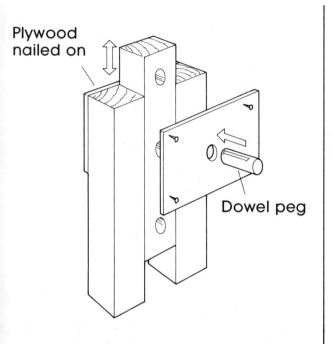

Plywood
nailed on

Dowel peg

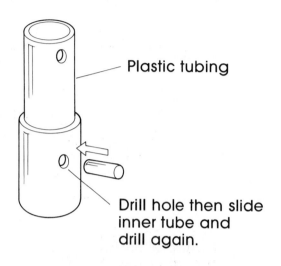

Plastic tubing

Drill hole then slide
inner tube and
drill again.

Choose tubes from a plumber's
supply shop that are a sliding fit.

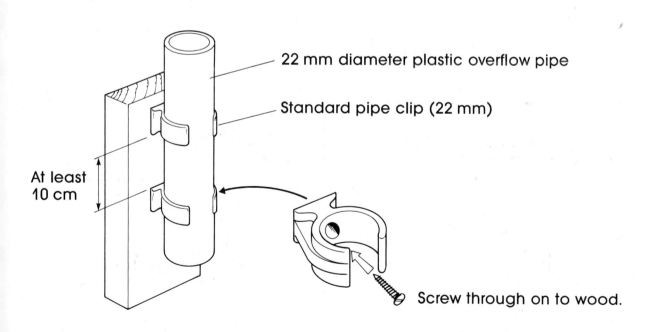

22 mm diameter plastic overflow pipe

Standard pipe clip (22 mm)

At least
10 cm

Screw through on to wood.

The pipe is held in position by friction.

Joining Corriflute 1

Score with a
blunt instrument.

Fold

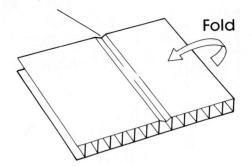

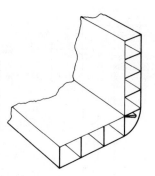

Cut carefully for
a neat corner.

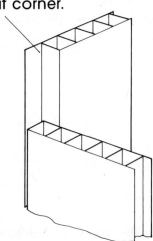

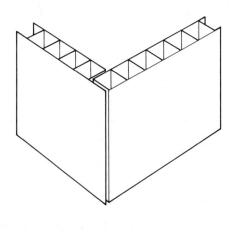

Dowel rod or coat hanger
wire doubled back

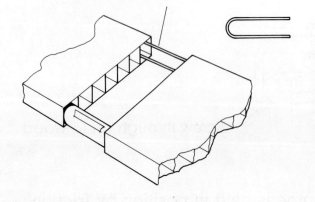

Bent coat hanger wire
doubled back

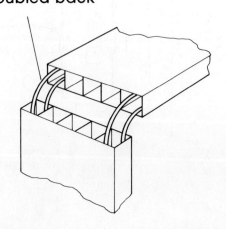

Joining Corriflute 2

This makes a good storage box or briefcase-style container.

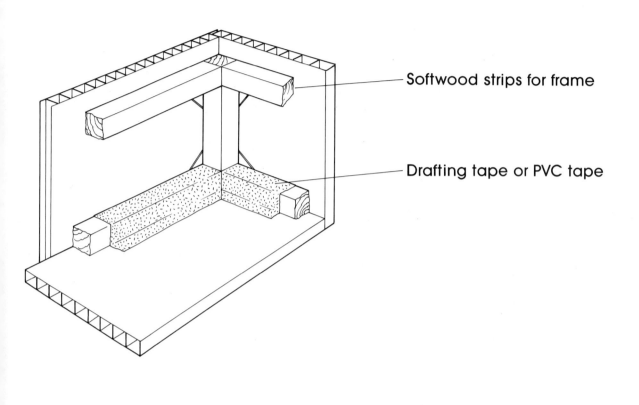

Softwood strips for frame

Drafting tape or PVC tape

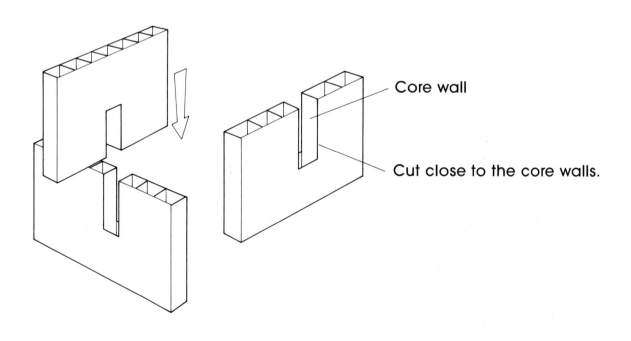

Core wall

Cut close to the core walls.

Boxes can be made with this method of joining.

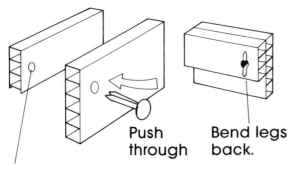

Make holes with Maun paper drill or screwdriver.

Push through

Bend legs back.

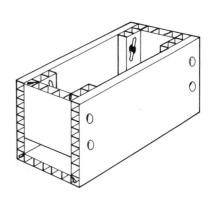

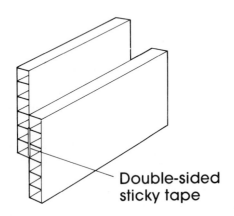

Double-sided sticky tape

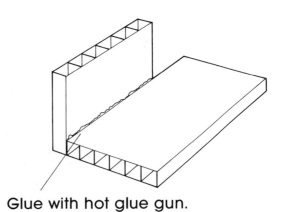

Glue with hot glue gun.

 Hot glue can burn.

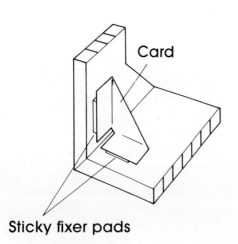

Card

Sticky fixer pads

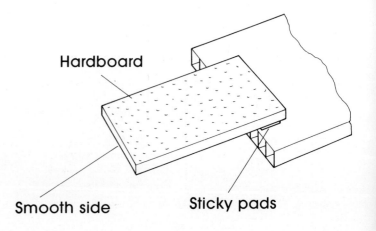

Hardboard

Smooth side

Sticky pads

Pivoting and hinging Corriflute

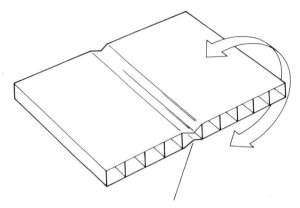

Score with blunt instrument
on both sides.

Single cut

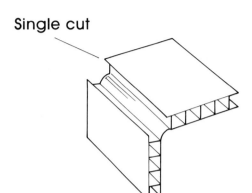

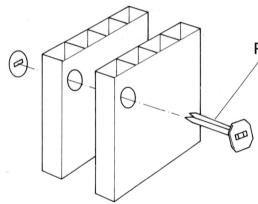

Premier Grip No. 644 and washer

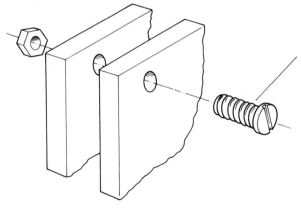

Nylon nut and bolt (expensive)

How to find the centre of a circle

Junk, such as margarine tub lids, jam and coffee jar lids, ready-cut card and plywood discs often need to be drilled or punched in the middle to fit wheel axles.

Here is an easy way to find the centre.

Draw round the disc.

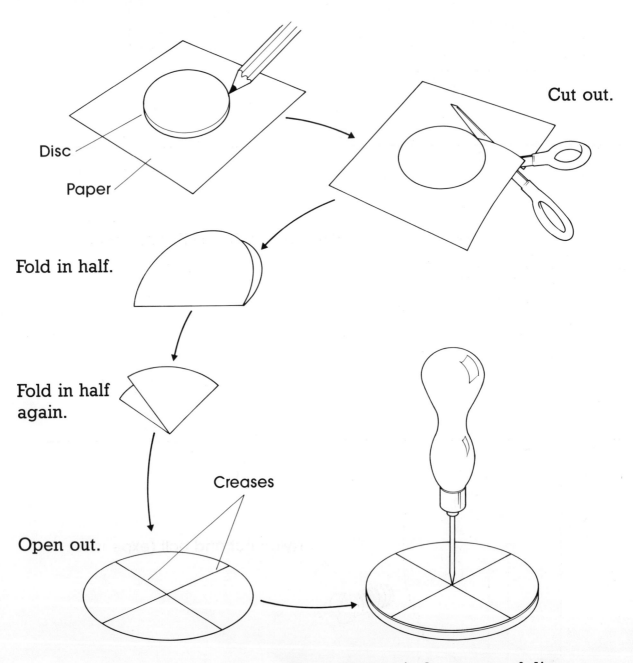

Disc

Paper

Cut out.

Fold in half.

Fold in half again.

Creases

Open out.

Place paper circle on top of disc.

Carefully mark through with a bradawl.

Rolling along 1

Adding simple wheels to axles and boxes

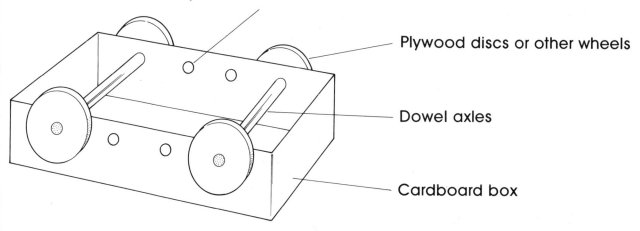

Use standard paper punch to make holes.

Plywood discs or other wheels

Dowel axles

Cardboard box

Another method of adding wheels

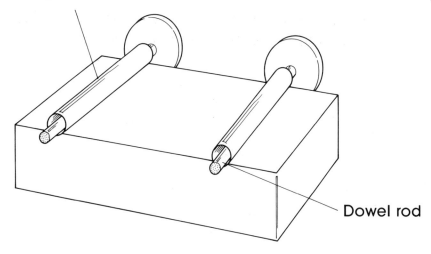

Jumbo Artstraws glued to box.
The dowel rod (diameter $4\frac{1}{2}$ mm)
spins freely inside.

Dowel rod

Instead of Artstraws you can use rolled cylinders of card or wooden beads fixed with hot glue.

Rolling along 2

Making a simple motor

1

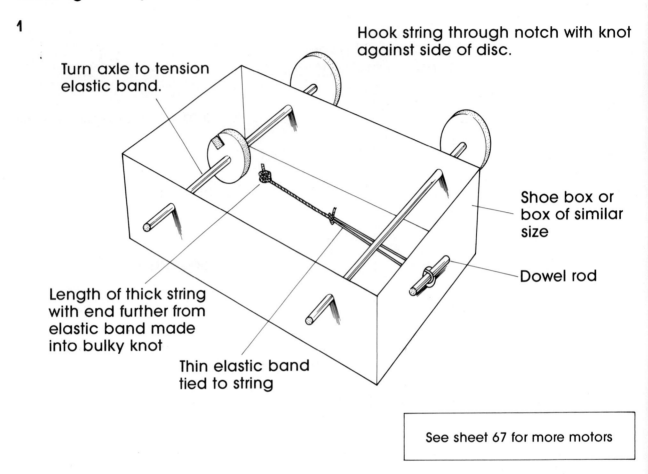

Turn axle to tension elastic band.

Hook string through notch with knot against side of disc.

Shoe box or box of similar size

Dowel rod

Length of thick string with end further from elastic band made into bulky knot

Thin elastic band tied to string

See sheet 67 for more motors

2 If the motor is put inside a shoe box the lid can be replaced. Then you can build on the lid and also get inside to the motor.

Going round and round

Wheels from plywood discs

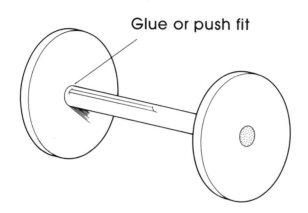

Glue or push fit

Glue two discs together
for a wide wheel.

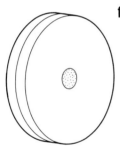

Glue three discs together
with smaller one in middle.

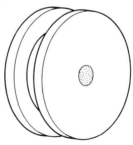

Drive band for vacuum cleaner
may fit and make a good tyre.

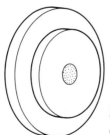

Stepped wheel suitable for
going along railway lines

Making wheels

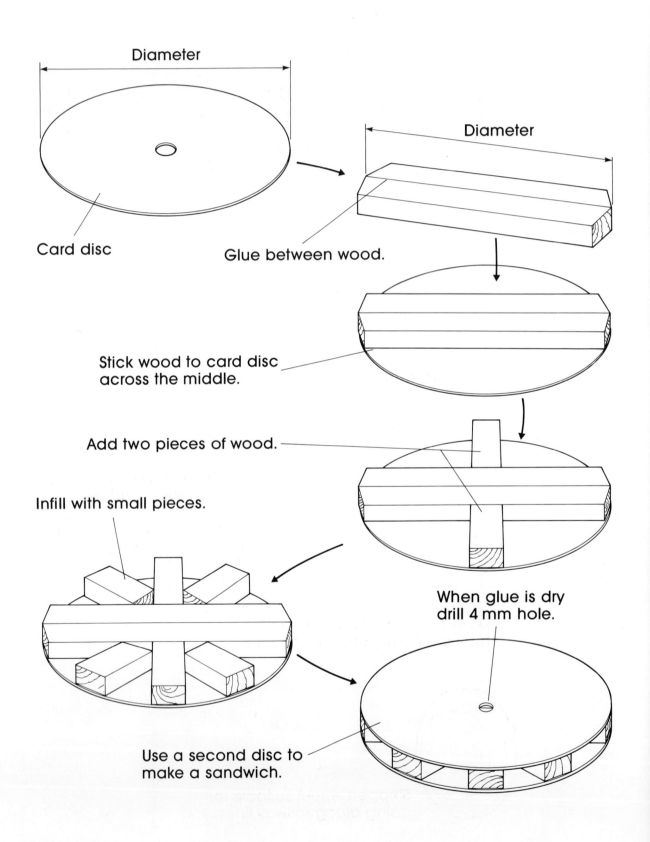

Diameter

Card disc

Glue between wood.

Diameter

Stick wood to card disc across the middle.

Add two pieces of wood.

Infill with small pieces.

When glue is dry drill 4 mm hole.

Use a second disc to make a sandwich.

Going round and round

Tyres and treads

Start with the wheel on sheet 49.

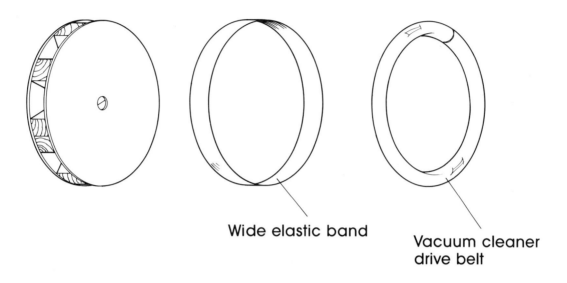

Wide elastic band

Vacuum cleaner
drive belt

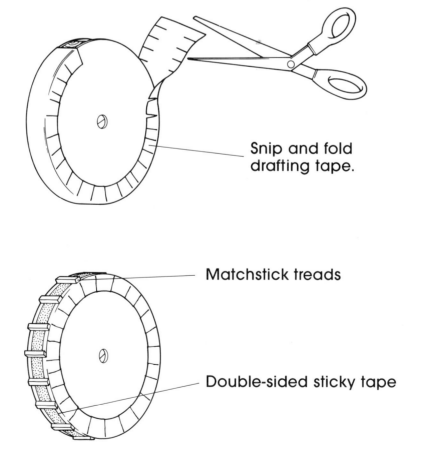

Snip and fold
drafting tape.

Matchstick treads

Double-sided sticky tape

Wheels for different conditions

Wheels for hard ground

On hard ground, thin wheels work well. You could use plywood discs, Corriflute or card. Some jam jar lids also work well. If the hard ground is smooth or polished, put an elastic band round the wheel for extra grip or traction.

Jam jar lid with elastic band tyre

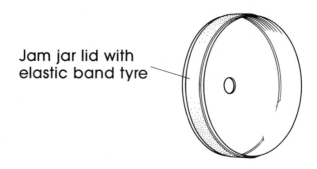

Wheels for soft ground

On soft ground, two other useful wheels are:

Coffee jar lids

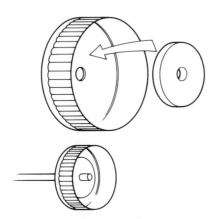

Make hole of diameter $4\frac{1}{2}$ mm or 5 mm in coffee jar lid.

Glue pre-drilled plywood disc to inside of lid after removing card and foil liner.

Ensure holes line up. Use hot glue gun for quick and easy gluing of wood to plastic.

Push $4\frac{1}{2}$ mm diameter dowel rod axle into hole in wooden disc as a tight fit.

Rollers made from plastic bottles or drink cans

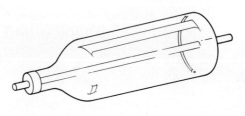

 Hot glue can burn.

1 To attach axles to frameworks use large card triangles.

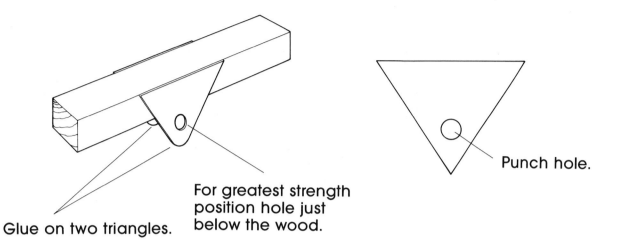

Glue on two triangles.

For greatest strength position hole just below the wood.

Punch hole.

See sheet 33 for card triangles

2 To be sure of a good fit and accurate line-up, you should put an axle through all the triangles and adjust their positions before the glue sticks them too firmly.

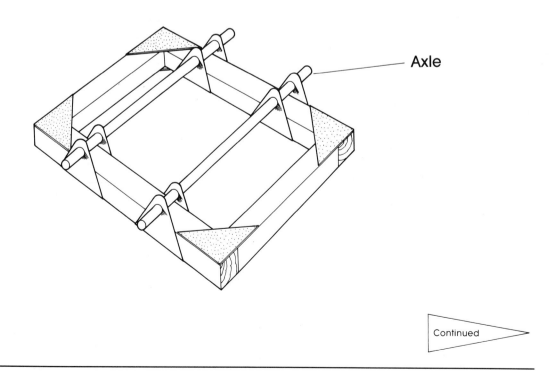

Axle

Continued

Going round and round

Axles and spindles 2

3 Axles fixed under the chassis make a stronger structure than those fitted above.

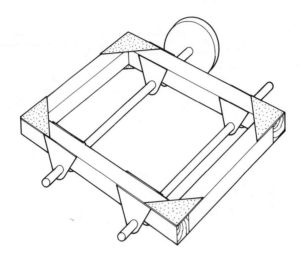

A vertically-mounted spindle

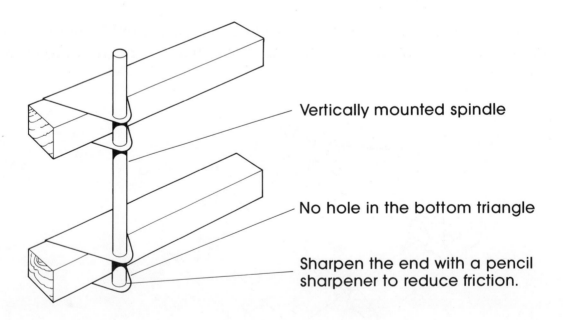

Vertically mounted spindle

No hole in the bottom triangle

Sharpen the end with a pencil sharpener to reduce friction.

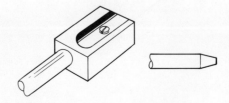

Pulleys and belts

Pulleys are a special kind of wheel. They can sometimes slip in use.

Make a small wheel
as on sheet 49.

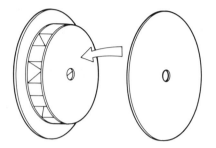

Glue two card discs
to the wheel.

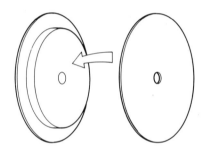

Plywood disc glued
between two card discs

Plastic pulley

How can you improve the grip between the pulley and the belt?

You can use elastic bands for drive belts.

Small elastic band     Large elastic band

To make larger drive belts use string tied to an elastic band.
This can make a drive belt of any length.

String tied to an elastic band

Rainbow Technology   Techniques for Primary Design and Technology   © 1991

Going round and round

Pulleys and power

A simple pulley system

When the crank handle is turned the driver pulley turns the driven pulley. The size of the pulleys is important. The driven pulley on the left goes slower than the driver but has more power. The driven pulley on the right goes faster but has less power.

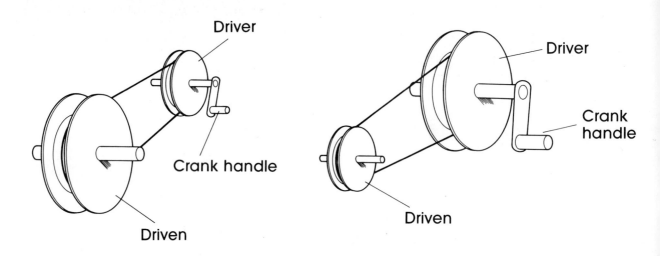

A complex pulley system

This pulley system gives a big decrease in speed but gains a huge increase in power.

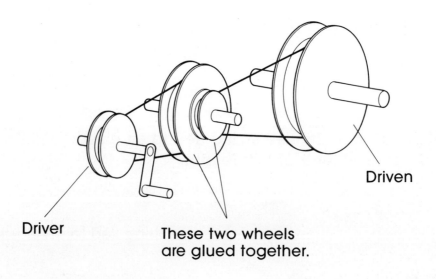

Gears

Gears are a special kind of wheel. They do not slip in use.

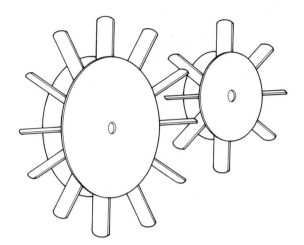

Edge-to-edge gearing
made with lollipop sticks

Two gears at right angles
made with matchsticks

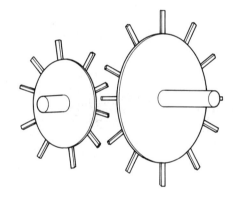

Symbols for gears

Symbol for a gear

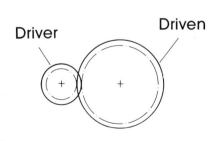

Driver

Driven

Speed reduction but power
increase

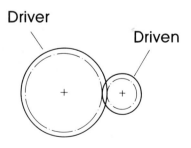

Driver

Driven

Speed increase but power
decrease

Making gears 1

1 If gears are to mesh together the distances between the gear teeth must be the same, whatever the size of the gears.

Make hole in centre of disc using handdrill or Maun paper drill.

These two distances should be the same at the edge of the card circles.

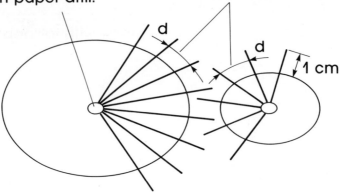

2 To make gears, use the templates on sheet 60 or use this method.

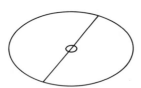

Card discs

Mark a line through the centre of each disc. Then make a trammel like this:

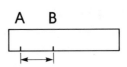

About 1 cm

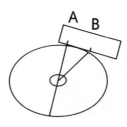

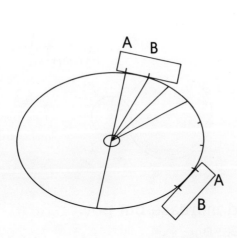

Use the trammel to mark off equal distances round the card discs.

Continued

Making gears 2

3 If, when you have marked all the way round, there is a gap left which is not the same as A to B, you must rub out the marks. Make A to B on the trammel a little smaller and try again.

Small gap left over

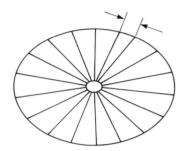

Old position of B

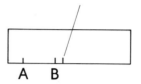

4 Glue two blocks of wood together. Then glue to the centre of the disc.

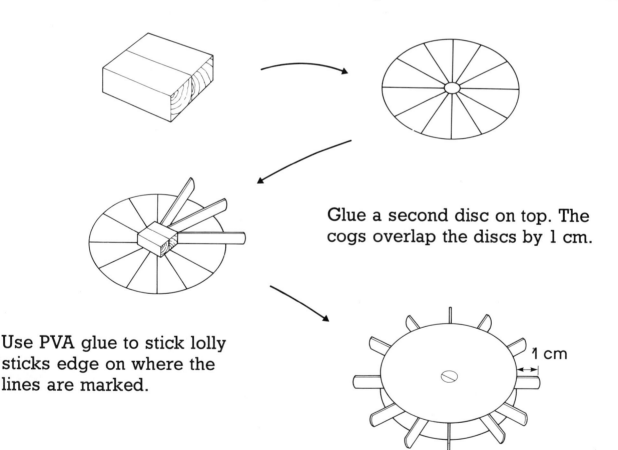

Glue a second disc on top. The cogs overlap the discs by 1 cm.

Use PVA glue to stick lolly sticks edge on where the lines are marked.

1 cm

Drill through centre of the gear wheel using the hole in the disc as a guide. Do not drill until the glue has dried thoroughly.

Making gears 3

To make right-angled gearing use matchsticks. Glue the matchsticks straight on to the card disc. Put another disc on top.

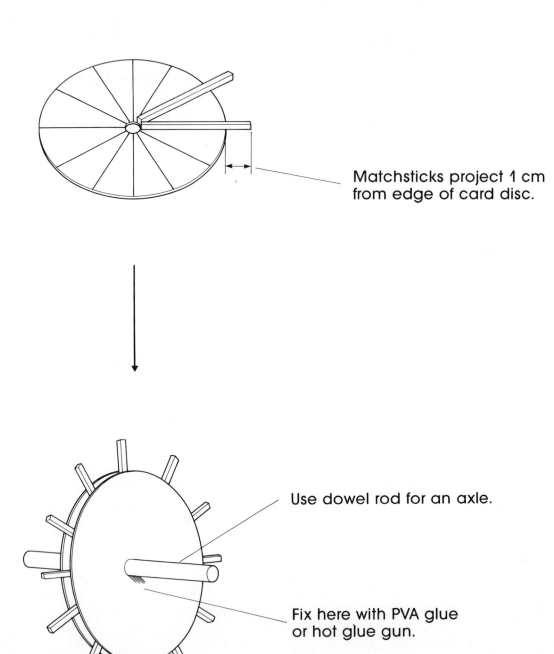

Matchsticks project 1 cm from edge of card disc.

Use dowel rod for an axle.

Fix here with PVA glue or hot glue gun.

⚠ Hot glue can burn.

Going round and round

Gear templates

10 teeth

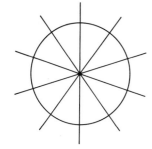

24 teeth

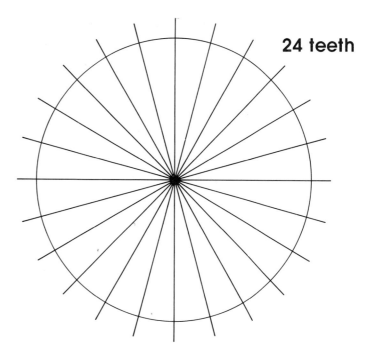

16 teeth

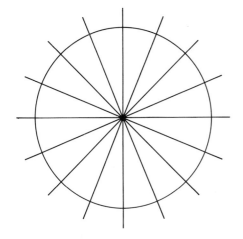

20 teeth

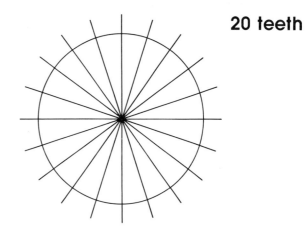

21 teeth

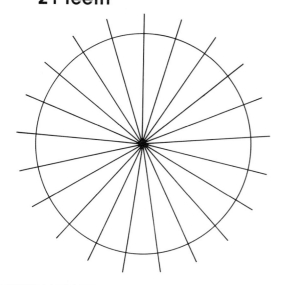

12 teeth

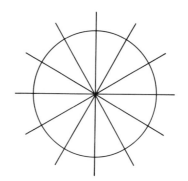

Winches and winding

A 35 mm film case winch

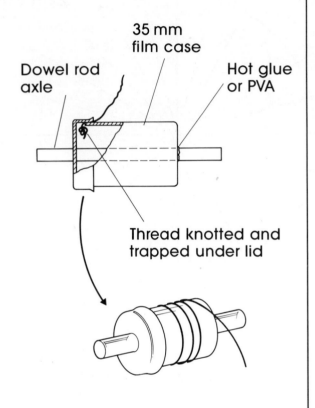

35 mm
film case

Dowel rod
axle

Hot glue
or PVA

Thread knotted and
trapped under lid

A wooden winch

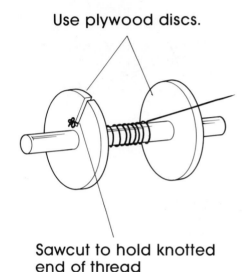

Use plywood discs.

Sawcut to hold knotted
end of thread

Crank handles

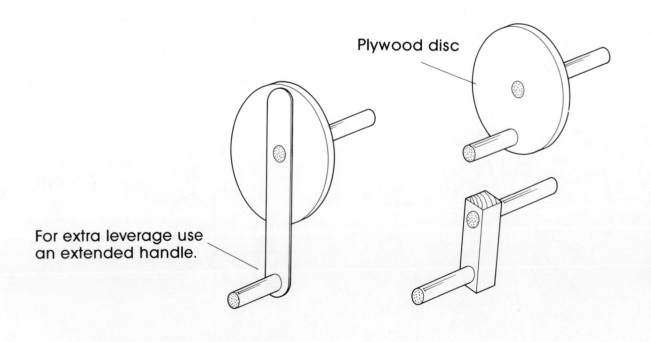

Plywood disc

For extra leverage use
an extended handle.

Turntables 1

Marble turntables

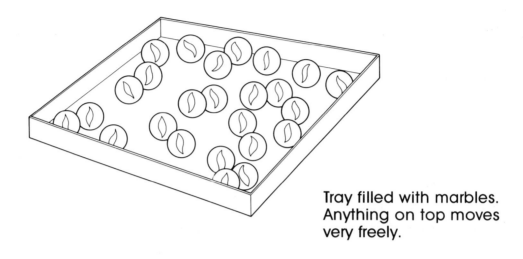

Tray filled with marbles. Anything on top moves very freely.

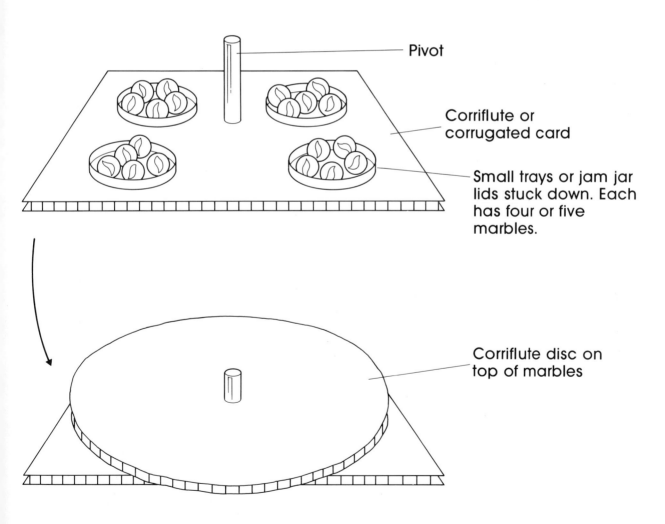

Pivot

Corriflute or corrugated card

Small trays or jam jar lids stuck down. Each has four or five marbles.

Corriflute disc on top of marbles

Turntables 2

A turntable from a toothpaste tube top

Toothpaste tube top with hole of diameter 3 mm drilled

4.5 mm diameter dowel rod slightly sharpened in a pencil sharpener

Press on a card disc with a hole in the middle. The disc should spin quite well.

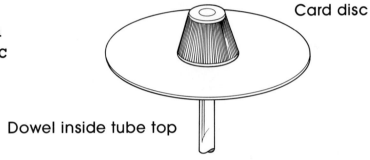

Card disc

Dowel inside tube top

A turntable from a washing up bottle

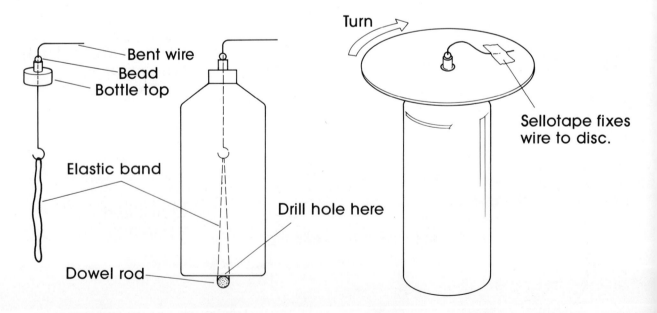

Bent wire
Bead
Bottle top

Elastic band

Dowel rod

Drill hole here

Turn

Sellotape fixes wire to disc.

Wind it up and let go!

Going round and round
Making turntables turn

Turning with a motor

This turntable can be used as a pulley for direct drive from a motor.

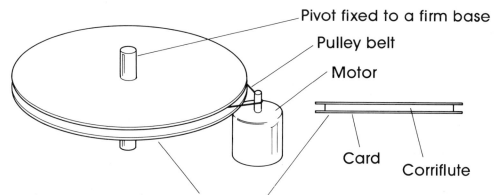

Pivot fixed to a firm base
Pulley belt
Motor
Card
Corriflute

Turntable with diameter about 30 cm made
as a sandwich of card discs with a Corriflute core

Corriflute of thickness up to 3 mm can be cut with good, strong kitchen
scissors. Protect pulley belt from uneven edges of corriflute disc by
wrapping in drafting tape.

> See sheet 50 for protective edge on disc
> See sheet 54 for pulley belt

Hand-cranked turntable

This crank turns motion through a right angle.

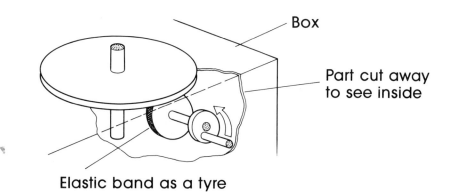

Box

Part cut away
to see inside

Elastic band as a tyre

A sideview of the mechanism

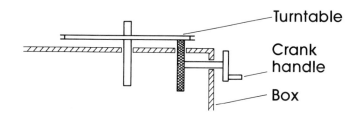

Turntable

Crank
handle

Box

65 Making noises
Noise makers

A rattling machine

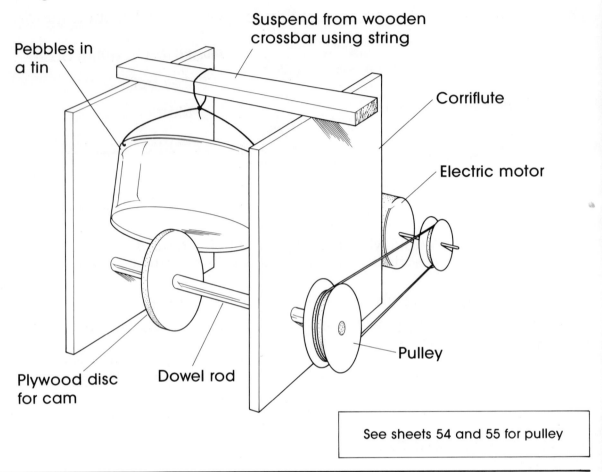

Pebbles in
a tin

Suspend from wooden
crossbar using string

Corriflute

Electric motor

Plywood disc
for cam

Dowel rod

Pulley

See sheets 54 and 55 for pulley

A clicking machine

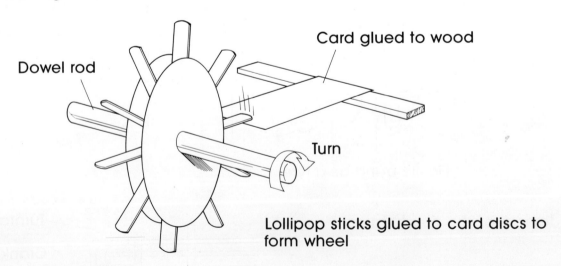

Dowel rod

Card glued to wood

Turn

Lollipop sticks glued to card discs to
form wheel

See sheets 56, 57 and 58 for wheel

Noises from stretched fibres

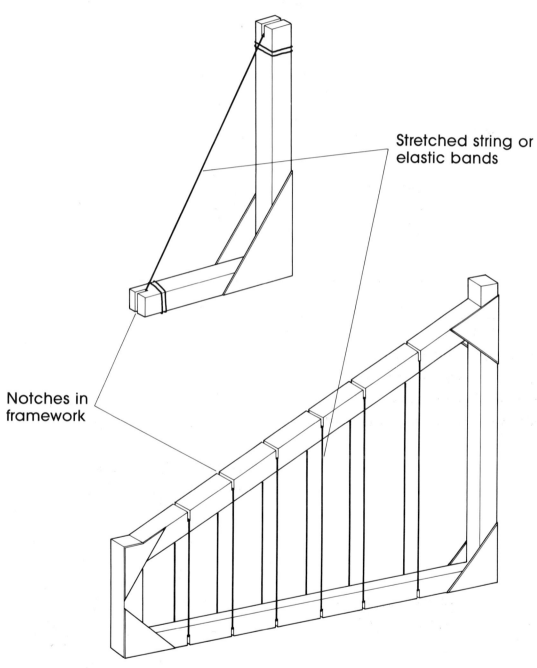

Stretched string or
elastic bands

Notches in
framework

Simple frameworks

See sheets 32, 33 and 34 for simple frameworks

Simple motors

An elastic band motor

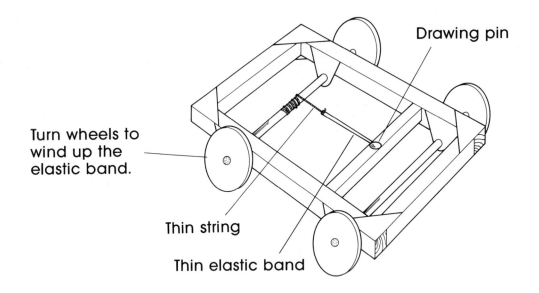

Drawing pin

Turn wheels to
wind up the
elastic band.

Thin string

Thin elastic band

A vertical engine

Using several pulleys with the elastic
band motor makes a difference to
the speed and power. Experiment
with different bands for different
results.

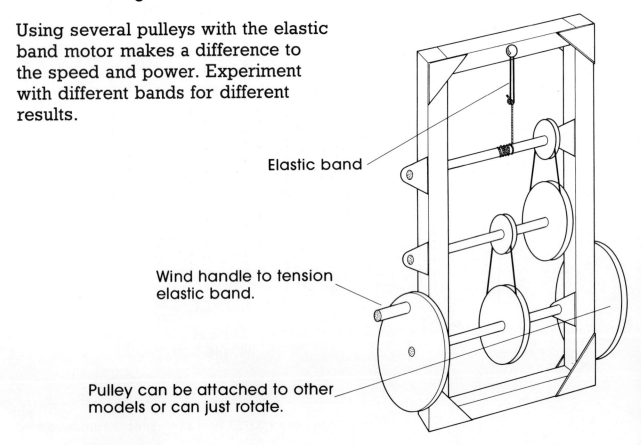

Elastic band

Wind handle to tension
elastic band.

Pulley can be attached to other
models or can just rotate.

Power from a falling weight 1

Models made from Lego or TEKO are easily powered by a falling weight.

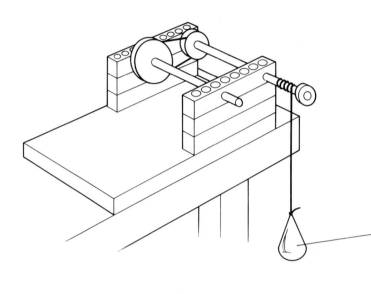

A fishing weight or similar

 Do not use lead.

Lego Technic or TEKO gears

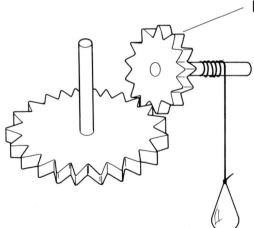

Motors

Power from a falling weight 2

The falling weight can be used to turn the axles and the wheels.

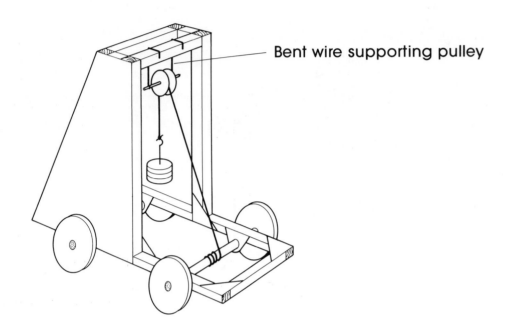

Bent wire supporting pulley

By using two pulleys, more turns of the axle can be achieved.

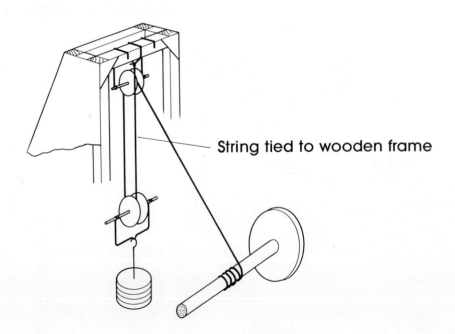

String tied to wooden frame

Power from balloons

If you blow up a balloon and let go it zooms about.

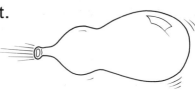

If you slow down the release of air you can use it to make a simple light vehicle move. To slow down the airflow, put a plug in the balloon with a small hole in it. The diameter of the plug or nozzle should be the same as that of the neck of the balloon.

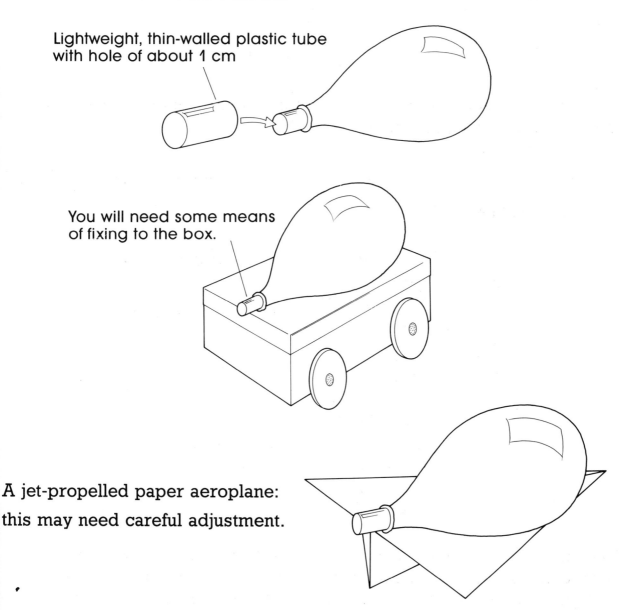

Lightweight, thin-walled plastic tube with hole of about 1 cm

You will need some means of fixing to the box.

A jet-propelled paper aeroplane:
this may need careful adjustment.

 ⚠ Personal hygiene – make sure you clean the nozzle before you blow.

Releasing

Release and trigger mechanisms 1

A wooden release

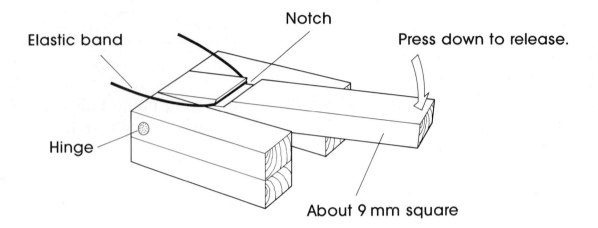

Elastic band   Notch   Press down to release.

Hinge

About 9 mm square

When the lever is pressed, the sides of the mechanism force the elastic band out of the notch until it is released.

A Lego motor release

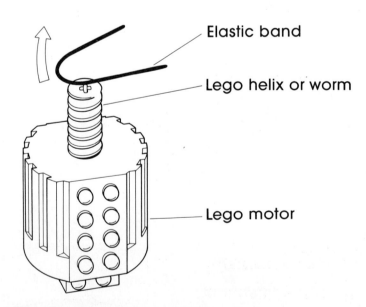

Elastic band

Lego helix or worm

Lego motor

When the motor is switched on, the elastic band runs up the helix or worm and is released provided the battery connections are suitably arranged. (A D.C. motor can be reversed by reversing the battery connections.)

Release and trigger mechanisms 2

Using water to trigger an electrical connection

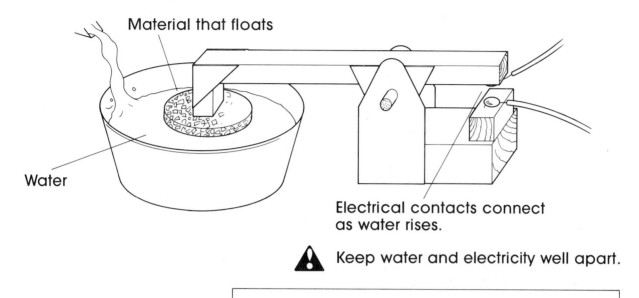

Material that floats

Water

Electrical contacts connect
as water rises.

⚠ Keep water and electricity well apart.

See sheet 4 for electrical connection using drawing pin

Using sand to trigger an electrical connection

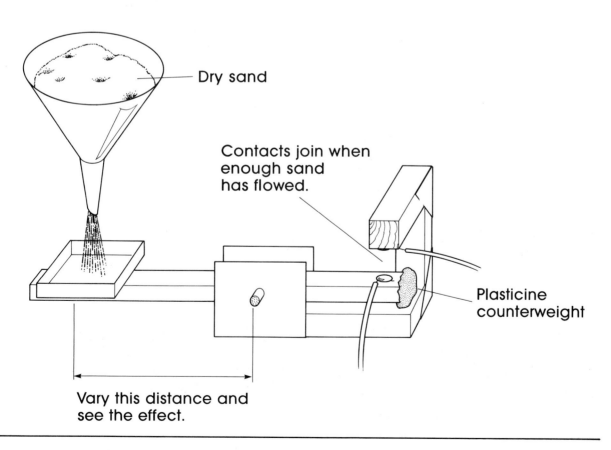

Dry sand

Contacts join when
enough sand
has flowed.

Plasticine
counterweight

Vary this distance and
see the effect.

Release and trigger mechanisms 3

Using a marble to trigger an electrical connection

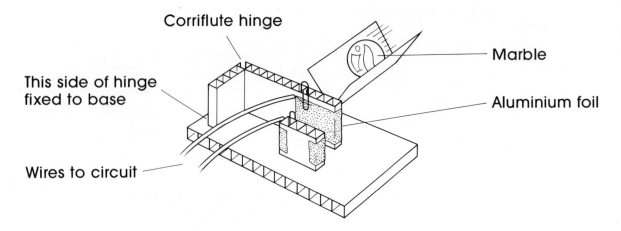

Corriflute hinge

Marble

This side of hinge
fixed to base

Aluminium foil

Wires to circuit

When the rolling marble hits the Corriflute hinge
the foil patches make contact.

See sheet **43** for joining Corriflute
See sheet **44** for Corriflute hinge

A brake for a vehicle

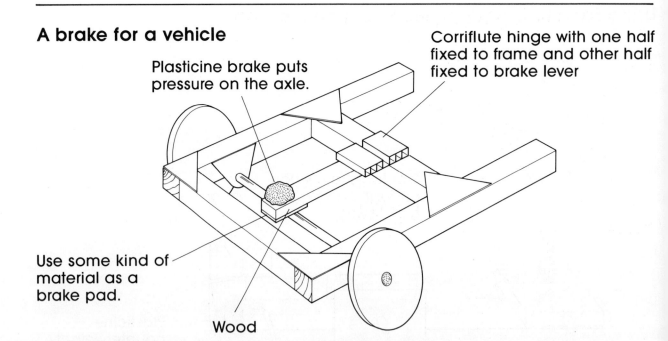

Plasticine brake puts
pressure on the axle.

Corriflute hinge with one half
fixed to frame and other half
fixed to brake lever

Use some kind of
material as a
brake pad.

Wood

You need to think of some way of moving the hinge so that the brake can
be put on and off.

Investigate a variety of brake pad materials such as cloth, pencil eraser,
leather, wood and hard plastic.

Release and trigger mechanisms 4

A release for an elastic band motor

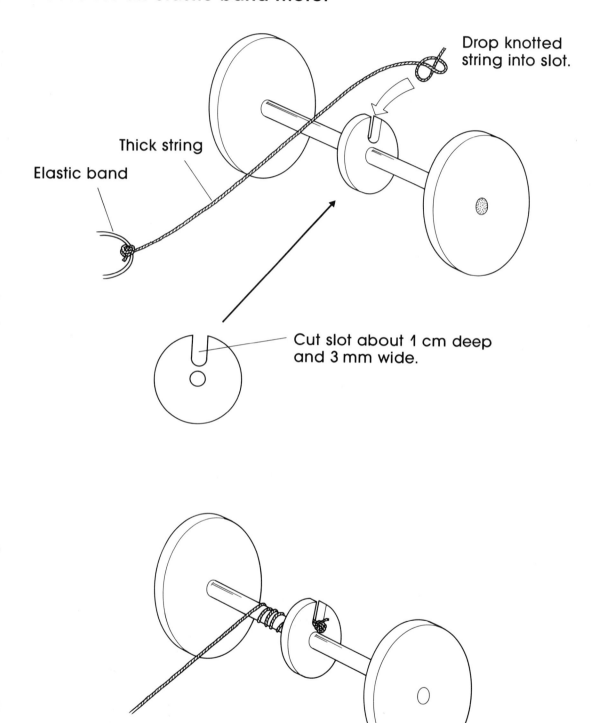

Drop knotted
string into slot.

Thick string

Elastic band

Cut slot about 1 cm deep
and 3 mm wide.

The string unwinds when pulled by the elastic band. The knotted end
pulls out of the slot and leaves the axle spinning freely.

One-way turning

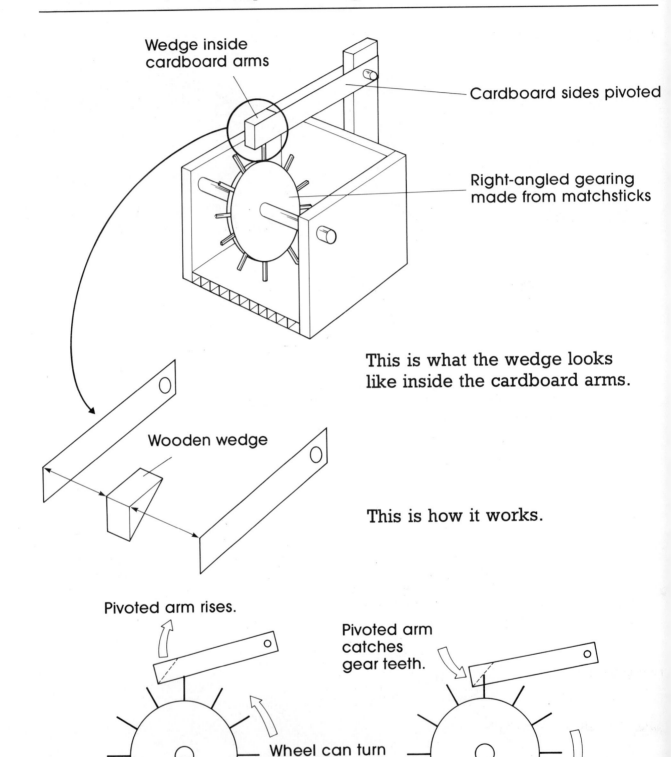

Wedge inside cardboard arms

Cardboard sides pivoted

Right-angled gearing made from matchsticks

This is what the wedge looks like inside the cardboard arms.

Wooden wedge

This is how it works.

Pivoted arm rises.

Pivoted arm catches gear teeth.

Wheel can turn this way.

Wheel cannot turn this way.

The wedge allows the gear to turn in one direction only.

Making adjustments
Sliding

A loose or easy fit

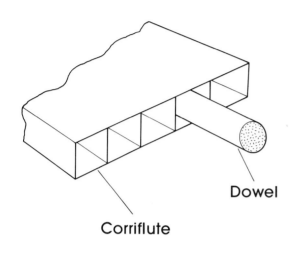

Dowel

Corriflute

A tight or friction fit

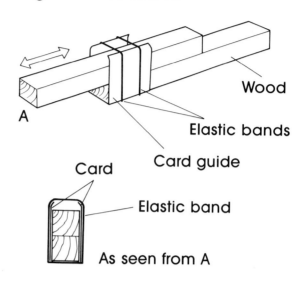

Wood

A

Elastic bands

Card guide

Card

Elastic band

As seen from A

Spring returns

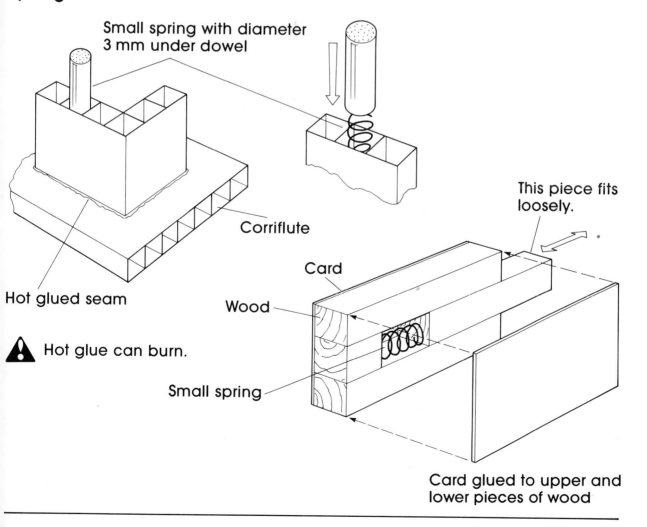

Small spring with diameter 3 mm under dowel

Corriflute

Hot glued seam

⚠ Hot glue can burn.

This piece fits loosely.

Card

Wood

Small spring

Card glued to upper and lower pieces of wood

Adjustable ladders 1

1 Make two ladders like this:

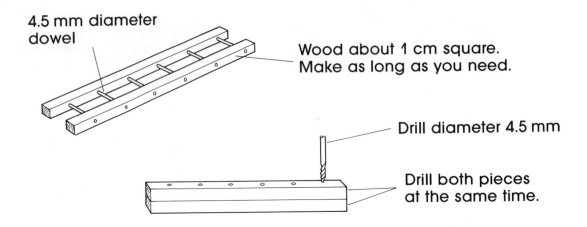

4.5 mm diameter dowel

Wood about 1 cm square. Make as long as you need.

Drill diameter 4.5 mm

Drill both pieces at the same time.

2

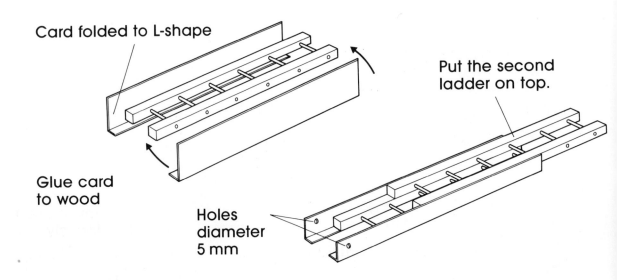

Card folded to L-shape

Put the second ladder on top.

Glue card to wood

Holes diameter 5 mm

3 Make a crank handle.

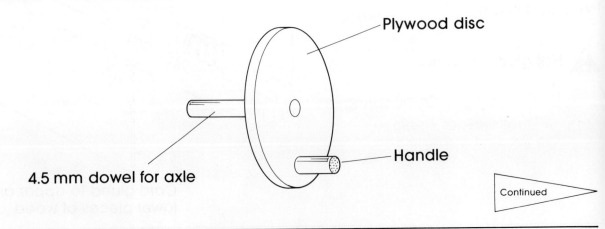

Plywood disc

Handle

4.5 mm dowel for axle

Continued

Adjustable ladders 2

4

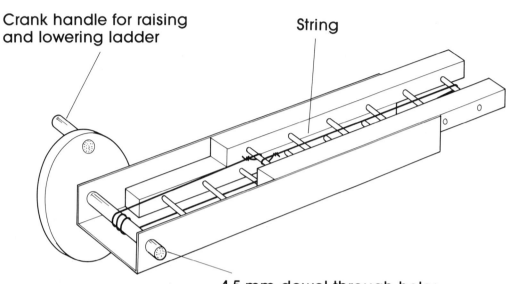

Crank handle for raising and lowering ladder

String

4.5 mm dowel through holes

5 Attach the string like this:

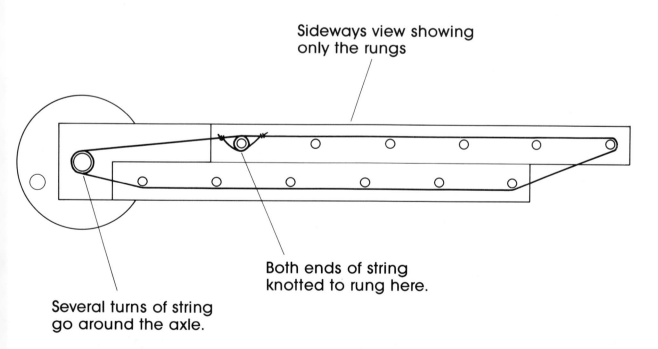

Sideways view showing only the rungs

Both ends of string knotted to rung here.

Several turns of string go around the axle.

Remote control linkages

A simple remote control linkage

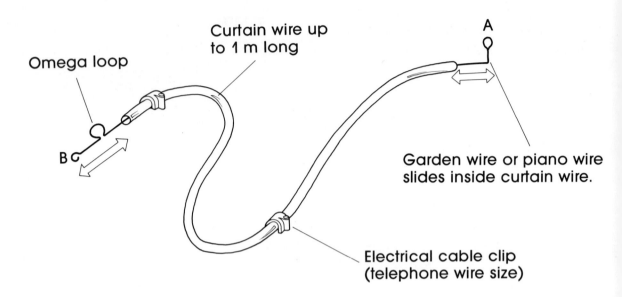

When A is moved B moves too. The omega loop is springy enough to allow for any excess strain and can prevent damage to whatever is being used at B.

A rocking bar

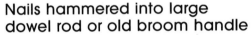

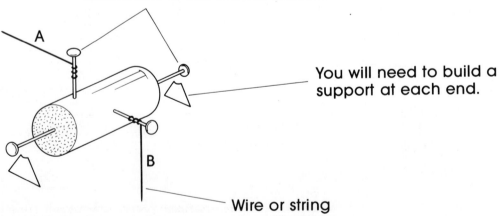

When A is moved back and forwards, B will move up and down. Rocking A enables a force in one direction to be turned through 90 degrees or round a corner.

Levers in models 1

A greetings card with a pendulum

Inside this card is a simple pendulum
that makes a ticking noise when
the card is gently rocked.

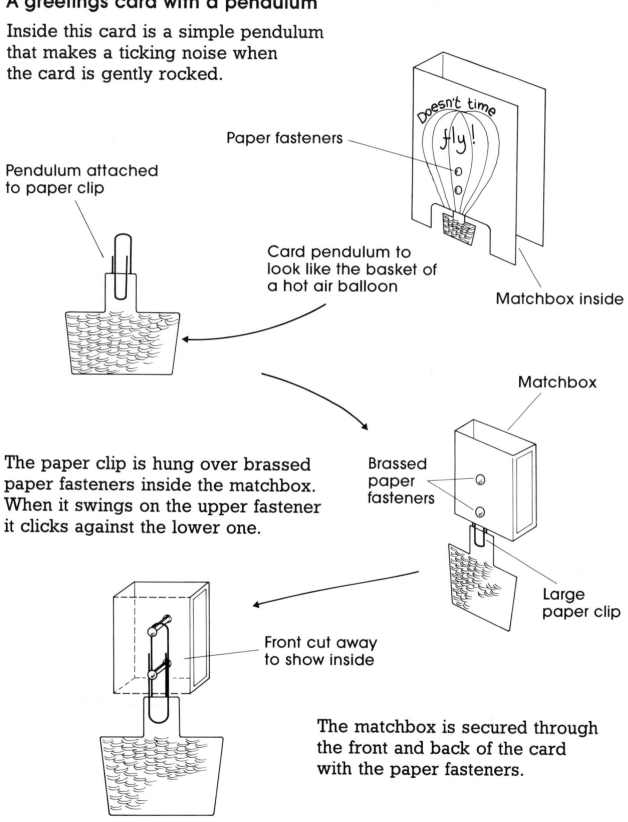

Paper fasteners

Doesn't time fly!

Pendulum attached
to paper clip

Card pendulum to
look like the basket of
a hot air balloon

Matchbox inside

Matchbox

The paper clip is hung over brassed
paper fasteners inside the matchbox.
When it swings on the upper fastener
it clicks against the lower one.

Brassed
paper
fasteners

Large
paper clip

Front cut away
to show inside

The matchbox is secured through
the front and back of the card
with the paper fasteners.

Levers in models 2

A greetings card with a falling weight mechanism

A clown card with a revolving bow tie

A dowel rod goes through the card to a pulley wheel at the back which has a length of thread with a weight on it. When the brake is taken off, the weight drops and the bow tie spins.

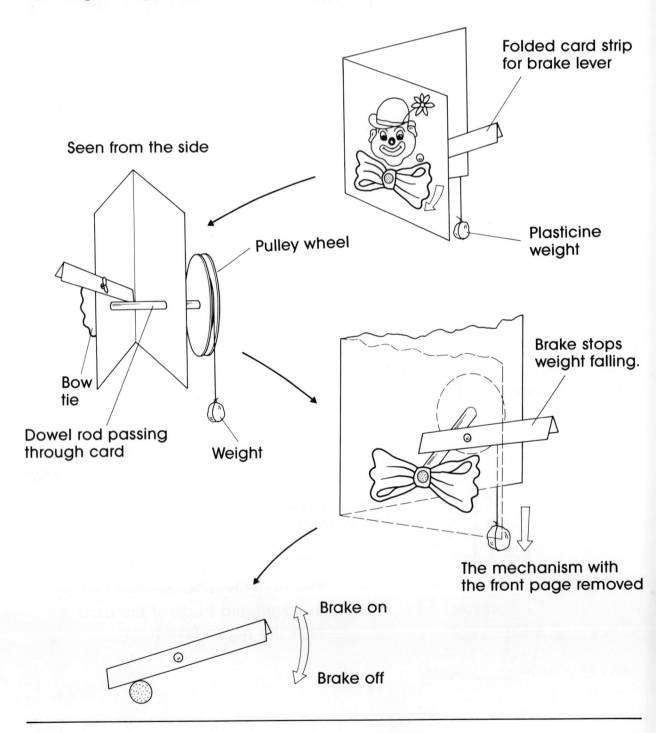

Seen from the side

Folded card strip for brake lever

Pulley wheel

Plasticine weight

Bow tie

Dowel rod passing through card

Weight

Brake stops weight falling.

The mechanism with the front page removed

Brake on

Brake off

Levers in models 3

Levers in greetings cards

1

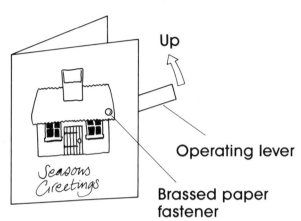

Up

Operating lever

Brassed paper fastener

Father Christmas appears.

Down

The lever system inside works like this. This is looking at the rear of the card front.

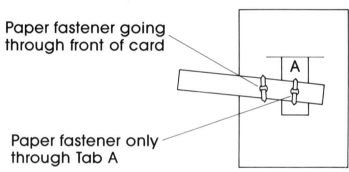

Paper fastener going through front of card

A

Paper fastener only through Tab A

2

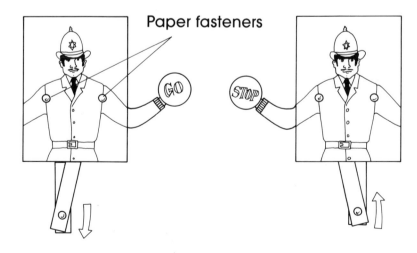

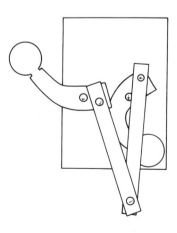

Paper fasteners

The lever system behind the card is more complicated.

Mechanisms

Simple mechanisms 1

Moving arms

The two arms move in and out but are always parallel.

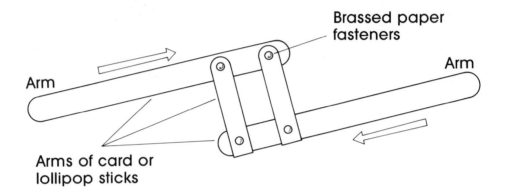

With this system the output is in the same direction as the input but it moves much further.

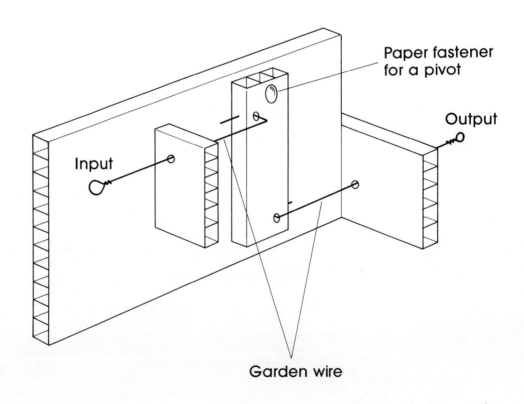

Simple mechanisms 2

Joining wires

Two ways of making flexible couplings:

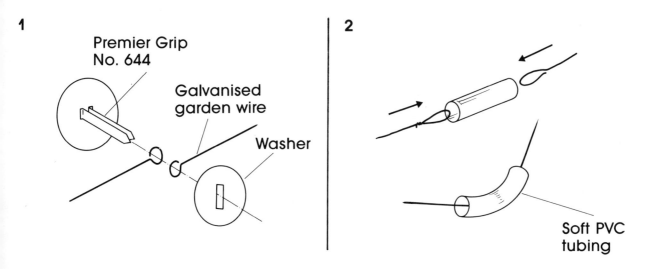

1

Premier Grip
No. 644

Galvanised
garden wire

Washer

2

Soft PVC
tubing

Cranks and connecting rods

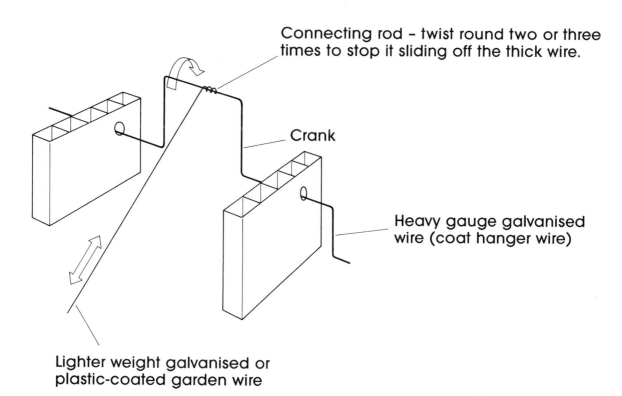

Connecting rod – twist round two or three
times to stop it sliding off the thick wire.

Crank

Heavy gauge galvanised
wire (coat hanger wire)

Lighter weight galvanised or
plastic-coated garden wire

When the handle is turned the connecting rod goes in and out.

Simple mechanisms 3

An improved crank

This crank works better with an eyelet as a bearing.

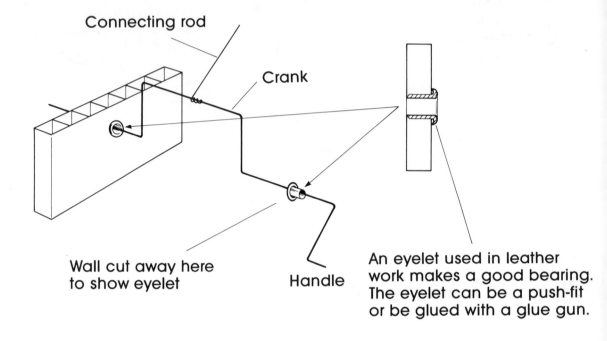

Connecting rod

Crank

Wall cut away here
to show eyelet

Handle

An eyelet used in leather
work makes a good bearing.
The eyelet can be a push-fit
or be glued with a glue gun.

Linking more cranks and connecting rods

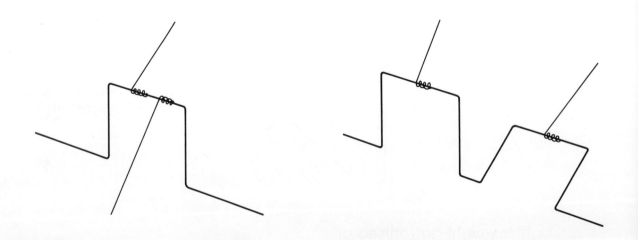

Two connecting rods can be
linked to one crank.

More than one crank can be used.

Simple mechanisms 4

Converting rotary to linear motion

This simple connection provides quite a violent movement. The connecting rod moves in an arc and goes up and down as well.

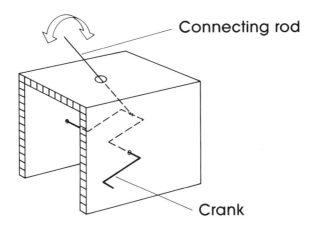

Connecting rod

Crank

This system converts the rotary motion of the handle into straight line motion that is vertical.

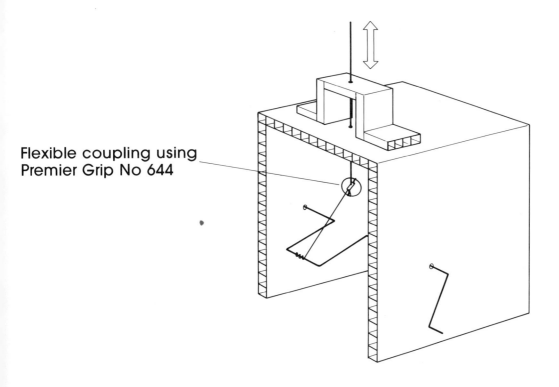

Flexible coupling using Premier Grip No 644

See sheet 84 for flexible coupling

Cams and eccentrics 1

Making an eccentric

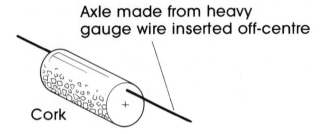

Axle made from heavy gauge wire inserted off-centre

Cork

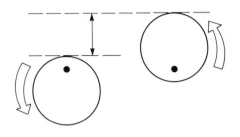

As the eccentric turns there is a rise and fall, as shown, between the dotted lines.

Cams

Cams can be made from thick card or thin plywood.

A snail cam

Cam followers move up and down with the cam

Snail cams give slow upwards ↑ and fast downwards ↓ motion.

A cardioid (heart-shaped) cam

Using a snail cam

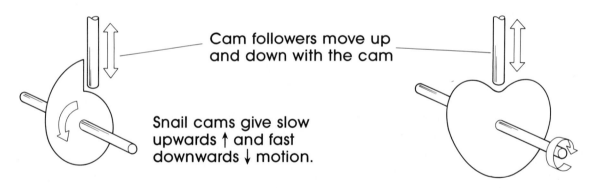

Dowel rod follower

Hat goes up and down

Clown's head seen from behind

Jumbo plastic straw about 4 cm long glued through top of box

An oval cam

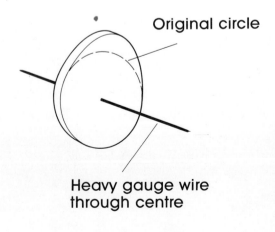

Original circle

Heavy gauge wire through centre

Cams and eccentrics 2

More eccentrics

1 Here is another way of using an eccentric to make a follower go up and down.

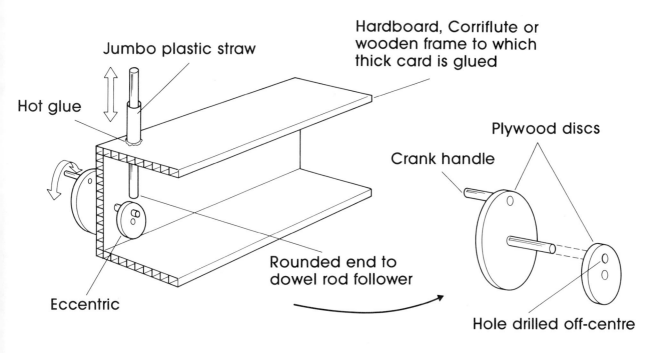

Jumbo plastic straw

Hardboard, Corriflute or wooden frame to which thick card is glued

Hot glue

Plywood discs

Crank handle

Rounded end to dowel rod follower

Eccentric

Hole drilled off-centre

2 You can attach a connecting rod to the eccentric. This moves up and down and backwards and forwards as the crank handle turns the eccentric.

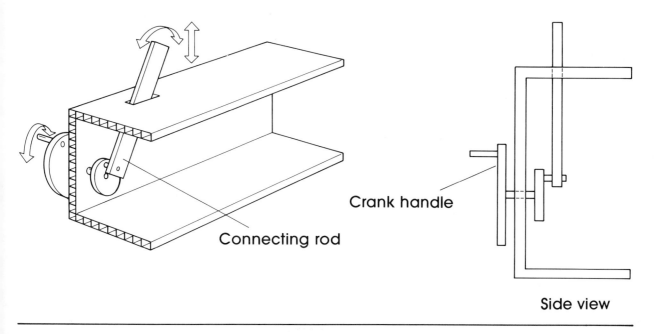

Crank handle

Connecting rod

Side view

Cranks and sliders

This crank is connected to a slider by a connecting rod which gives a straight up and down action like the piston in an engine.

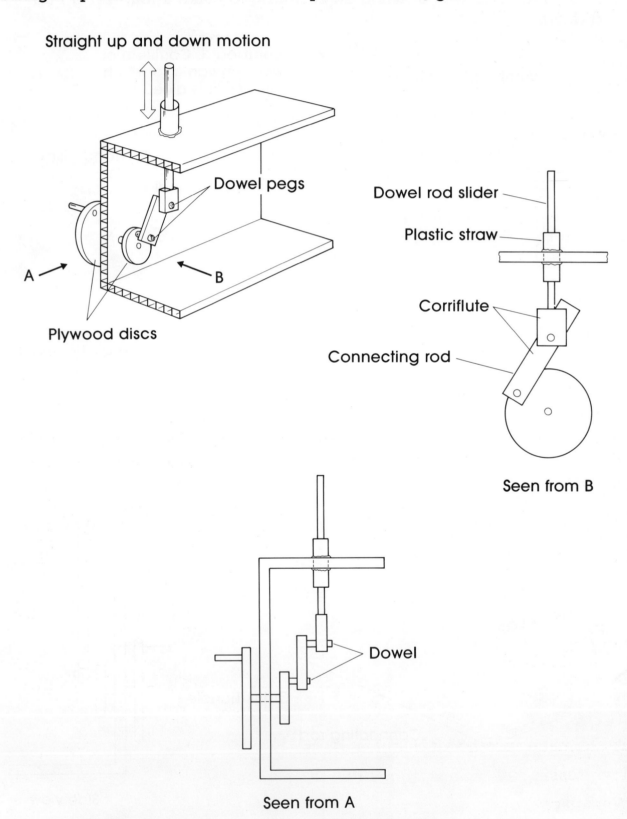

Straight up and down motion

Dowel pegs

Plywood discs

A

B

Dowel rod slider

Plastic straw

Corriflute

Connecting rod

Seen from B

Dowel

Seen from A

Making pneumatic and hydraulic systems 1

Pneumatic systems

Pneumatic systems are air filled.

1 Connect two syringes of the same size with plastic tubing.

Try pressing the plungers on the syringes together and separately. What happens?

2 Connect two syringes of different volume. Try pressing the plungers together and separately. What happens now?

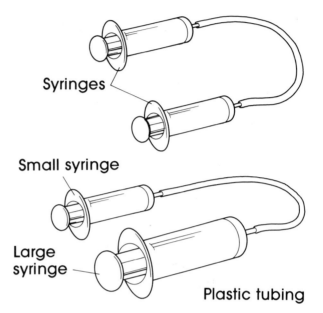

Syringes

Small syringe

Large syringe

Plastic tubing

Hydraulic systems

Hydraulic systems are water filled.

1 To make a hydraulic system, fill the first pneumatic system above like this:

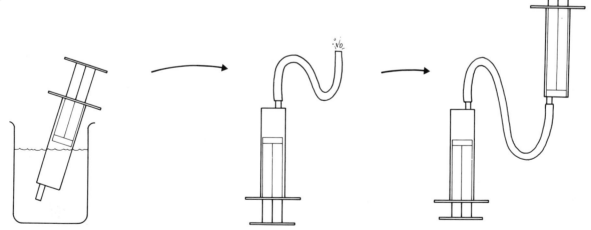

Fill one syringe

Attach tubing and press syringe enough to fill tube.

Attach another syringe with plunger fully depressed.

Try to make sure no air bubbles get in.

Try pressing the plungers together and separately.

What happens?

Continued

Making pneumatic and hydraulic systems 2

2 Make a hydraulic system with a large and a small syringe. Set up a length of wood on a table. Try pressing the large syringe. What happens? Change the syringes over. What happens now?

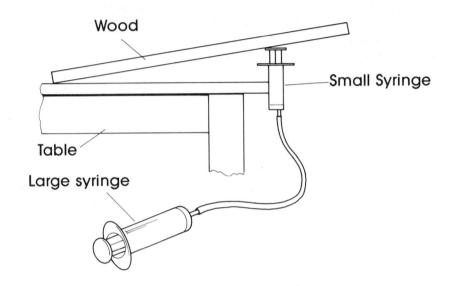

3 A T-piece allows two small syringes to work at the same time, when a large syringe is pressed. Use 10 ml and 20 ml syringes as shown.

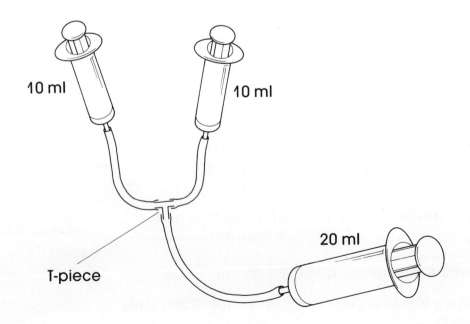

Using a pneumatic or hydraulic system

A lifting ladder on a fire engine

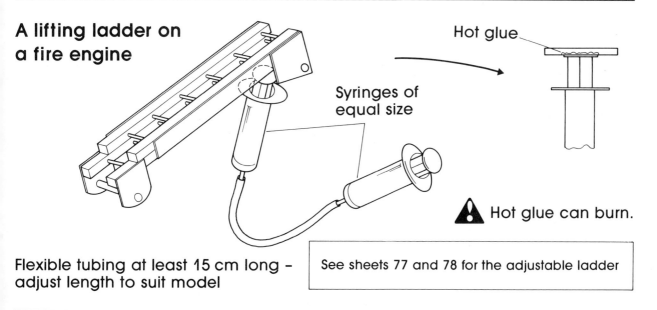

Hot glue

Syringes of equal size

⚠ **Hot glue can burn.**

Flexible tubing at least 15 cm long – adjust length to suit model

See sheets 77 and 78 for the adjustable ladder

Moving a toy

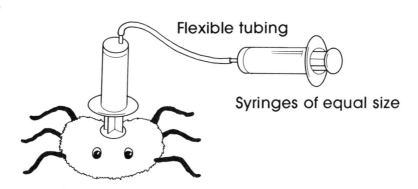

Flexible tubing

Syringes of equal size

A spider going up or down or backwards or forwards

A lifting bridge

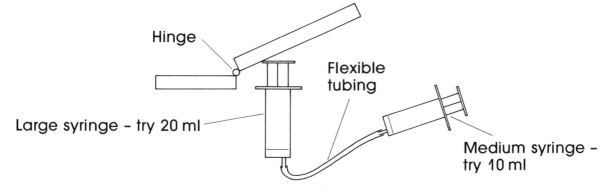

Hinge

Flexible tubing

Large syringe – try 20 ml

Medium syringe – try 10 ml

Parts of the bridge are easily made with Corriflute or corrugated cardboard.

Adjusting hydraulic systems

A self-returning system

Simple hydraulic systems are a nuisance when you have to push the syringe in and then pull it out.

Cut notches in the syringe with a file. The arrows mark the four notches needed.

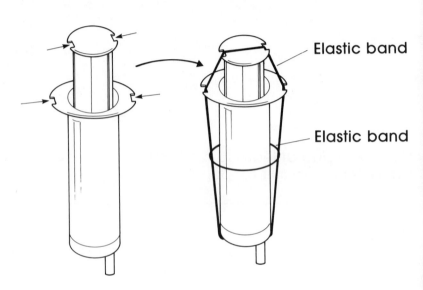

Elastic band

Elastic band

Locking a self-returning system

If you want to keep a syringe closed you can make a lock.

Plastic pipe clips from a plumber's store

Corriflute hinge glued securely to baseboard. When the flap is raised, the syringe cannot return, when lowered it can.

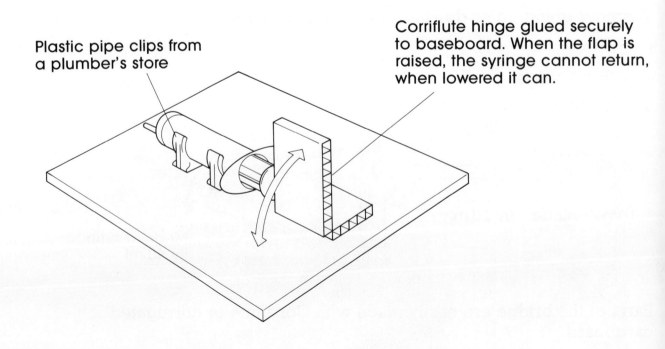

A simple hydraulic valve

A simple valve can be made to control a hydraulic system. If the tube is squeezed then no water can move when the syringe is pressed. A lolly stick can be used to squeeze the tube as follows:

1

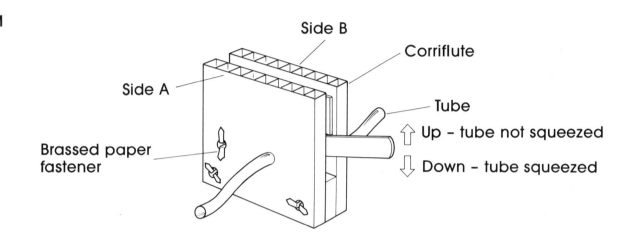

Side B

Corriflute

Side A

Tube

⇧ Up – tube not squeezed

⇩ Down – tube squeezed

Brassed paper fastener

2 A cut-away view will show how the valve is made. Side A is not shown.

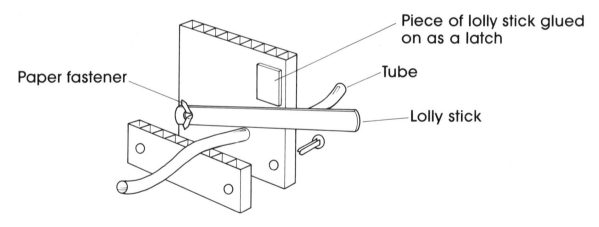

Piece of lolly stick glued on as a latch

Paper fastener

Tube

Lolly stick

3 The valve is used like this:

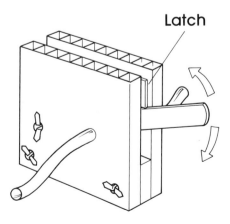

Latch

Press down to squeeze tube. The lolly stick can be held under the latch glued to the Corriflute. Press up to release.

Hammer and nails

1 Nails come in various shapes and lengths. Try to choose the most suitable for your task.

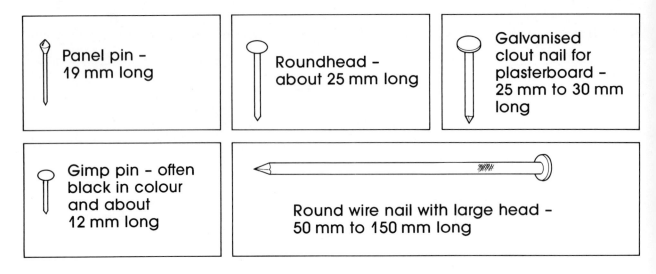

Panel pin – 19 mm long

Roundhead – about 25 mm long

Galvanised clout nail for plasterboard – 25 mm to 30 mm long

Gimp pin – often black in colour and about 12 mm long

Round wire nail with large head – 50 mm to 150 mm long

If you have not used nails before use a long one with a biggish head.

2 Here are some ways of keeping the nail upright without bruising your fingers.

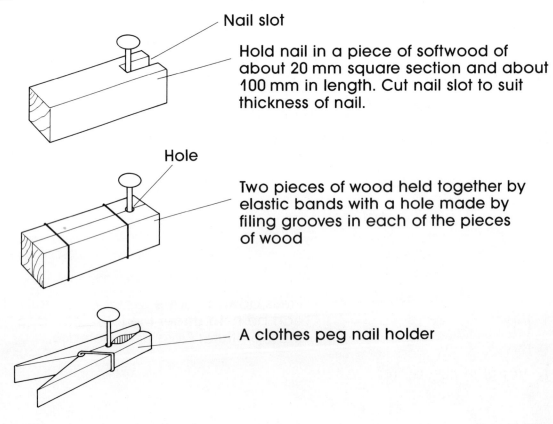

Nail slot

Hold nail in a piece of softwood of about 20 mm square section and about 100 mm in length. Cut nail slot to suit thickness of nail.

Hole

Two pieces of wood held together by elastic bands with a hole made by filing grooves in each of the pieces of wood

A clothes peg nail holder

Rainbow Technology   Techniques for Primary Design and Technology   © 1991

Fastening with everyday bits and pieces 1

Pipe clips

1 Pipe clips can be bought from DIY and plumber's stores to suit 15 mm or 22 mm diameter pipes.

Screw hole

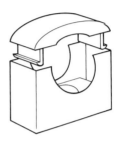

2 They are useful for holding round things such as syringes and motors.

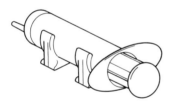

Motors and syringes that are too small can be wrapped with Sellotape.

3 For a more permanent fixing a little hot glue can be used.

 Hot glue can burn.

Continued

Fastening with everyday bits and pieces 2

4 Two clips can be joined with an M4 nut and bolt to make a swivel joint.

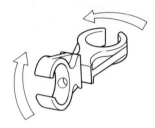

5 Clips can be screwed to wooden blocks.

6 Terry clips can also be used to hold round things.

   — Elastic band for extra grip

Bulldog clips

These have many uses.

Holding materials together
while the glue dries

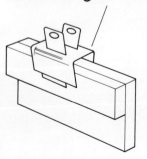

Holding wood next to
an aluminium food tray

Fastening with everyday bits and pieces 3

Overflow pipes and bends

1 Overflow pipes and bends are friction fits and can make strong frameworks. The pipe has 22 mm diameter.

Pipe or dowel rod

2 T-connectors are also good for structures.

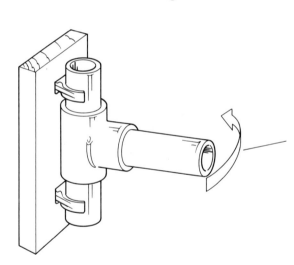

Pipe clips, pipe and a T-connector make a towel rail that swings away for storage.

Empty felt tip pens

Empty felt tip pens make good conveyor belt supports.

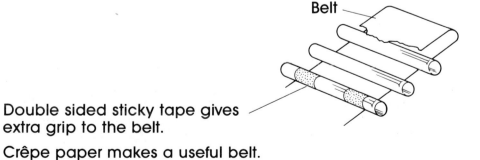

Belt

Double sided sticky tape gives extra grip to the belt.

Crêpe paper makes a useful belt.

Making hinges 1

Corriflute hinges

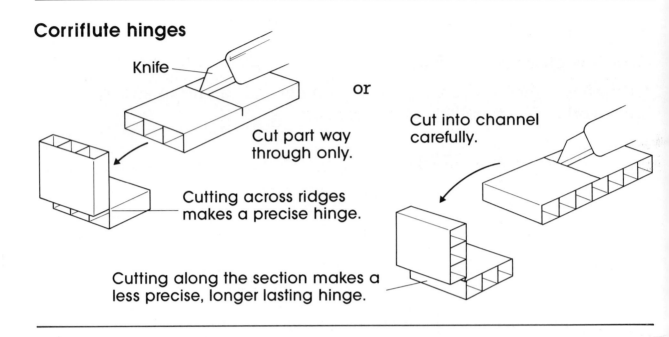

Knife

Cut part way through only.

or

Cut into channel carefully.

Cutting across ridges makes a precise hinge.

Cutting along the section makes a less precise, longer lasting hinge.

Cotton cloth hinges

Use PVA glue on paper or card and allow it to dry thoroughly. Contact adhesive will be needed on Corriflute.

Plastic hinges

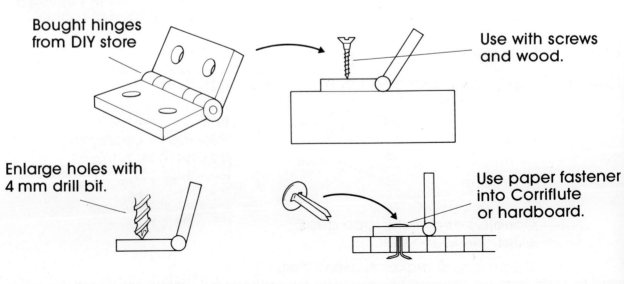

Bought hinges from DIY store

Use with screws and wood.

Enlarge holes with 4 mm drill bit.

Use paper fastener into Corriflute or hardboard.

Making hinges 2

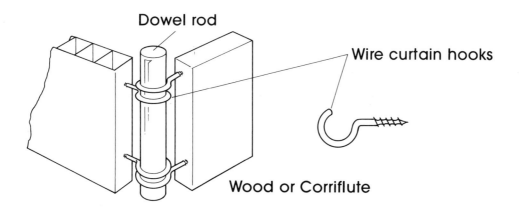

Dowel rod

Wire curtain hooks

Wood or Corriflute

Corriflute can be used with dowel rod or Plawcotech rods.

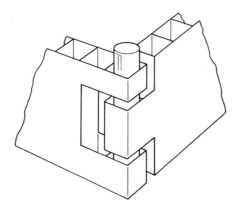

Several layers of Sellotape can make a light duty hinge.

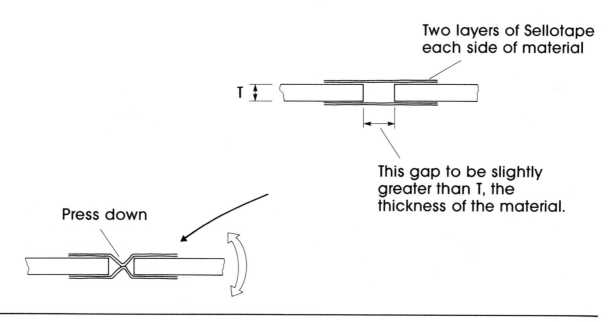

Two layers of Sellotape each side of material

This gap to be slightly greater than T, the thickness of the material.

Press down

A pinhole camera

Take a 110 mm film cassette.

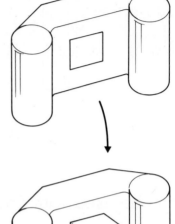

Attach a box with a pinhole in it.

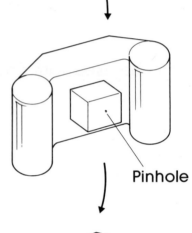

Pinhole

The box must be painted matt black inside and be fastened on so that no light can get in – use black insulating tape.

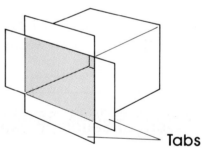

Tabs

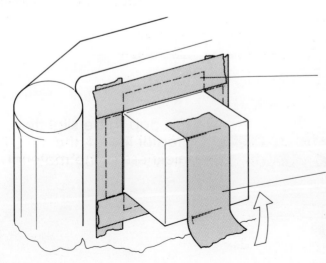

Tabs stuck down with black insulating tape

Sticky tape shutter. Pull tape up to let light into the pinhole.

A home-made construction set 1

This home-made construction set will provide you with a cheap and highly flexible resource for making up structures and models.

For the construction set you will need:

- 10 lengths of dowel rod 300 mm long × 5 mm diameter

- 10 lengths of dowel rod 150 mm long × 5 mm diameter

- 4 plastic golf balls

- A handful of small elastic bands

- Several short lengths of galvanised steel garden wire (less than 15 cm long) of diameter less than 1 mm

- Some washers with inside diameter about 5 mm

- An A4 size cardboard box to store the set

- A length of thick-walled plastic or rubber tube cut into short lengths. (Wine-making tubing is ideal.) Inside diameter to be a tight fit on the dowel rod.

Continued ▶

A home-made construction set 2

Basic structures can be made up with the dowel rod as follows:

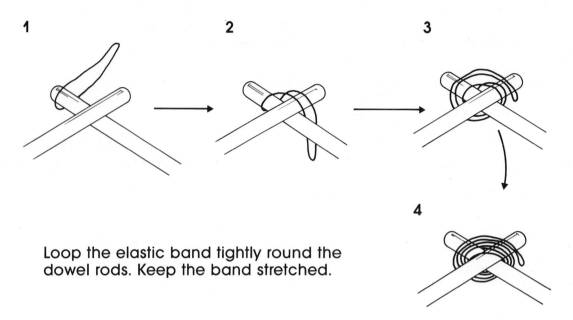

1   **2**   **3**

4

Loop the elastic band tightly round the dowel rods. Keep the band stretched.

Depending on how carefully the rods are lashed, the angle between the dowel rods can be varied:

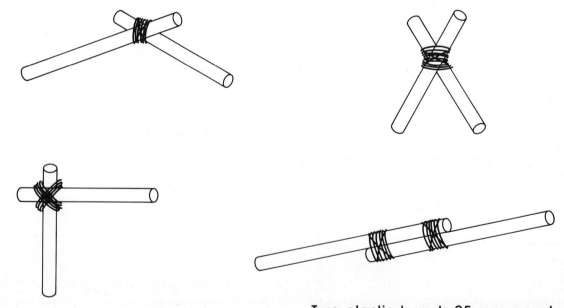

Two elastic bands 25 mm apart will join two rods in a firm, straight way.

Continued

Construction set

A home-made construction set 3

Other features can be added:

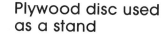

Plywood disc used
as a stand

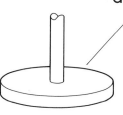

The golfballs have a hole diameter
of 6 mm and are a good running
fit on 5 mm diameter rod.

They can be used for wheels
on axles.

Flexible tube cut 3 mm long –
inside diameter to suit dowel
rod and to be a tight fit.

The galvanised steel garden wire
can be used for fixings too.

Galvanised steel
garden wire

Hold on with
rubber bands

A swinging arm

Galvanised steel wire
or a straightened
paper clip

Washer

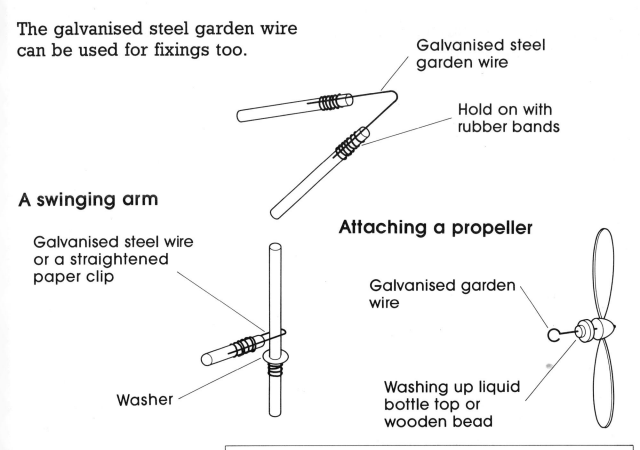

Attaching a propeller

Galvanised garden
wire

Washing up liquid
bottle top or
wooden bead

See sheet 29 for structures to make with the construction set